PAUL BANE
MATT LITTON

IN THE
PRESENCE
OF
JESUS

*A 40-Day Guide to the Intimacy with God
You've Always Wanted*

TYNDALE
MOMENTUM®

A Tyndale nonfiction imprint

Visit Tyndale online at tyndale.com.

Visit Tyndale Momentum online at tyndalemomentum.com.

Tyndale, Tyndale's quill logo, *Tyndale Momentum*, and the Tyndale Momentum logo are registered trademarks of Tyndale House Ministries. Tyndale Momentum is the nonfiction imprint of Tyndale House Publishers, Carol Stream, Illinois.

In the Presence of Jesus: A 40-Day Guide to the Intimacy with God You've Always Wanted

Designed by Jennifer Phelps

Published in association with the literary agency of Legacy, LLC, Winter Park, Florida 32789.

For information about special discounts for bulk purchases, please contact Tyndale House Publishers at csresponse@tyndale.com, or call 1-855-277-9400.

Library of Congress Cataloging-in-Publication Data

A catalog record for this book is available from the Library of Congress.

ISBN 978-1-4964-5562-8

Printed in the United States

27 26 25 24 23 22
7   6   5   4   3

To my beautiful Cathy

PAUL BANE

———————————————┼———————————————

For LL

MATT LITTON

Contents

Introduction

After thirty years of full-time ministry, I had arrived at a moment of desperation. I still recall pulling up a chair in the solitude of my study to take an honest inventory of my life as a Christian and as a pastoral leader. I had done all the "right things" that I'd been taught to do, but still I found myself burned out, weary, and frankly, I just didn't sense the presence of Christ in my life. Yes, I had spent my days talking about God and had dedicated my life to serving Him, but I still felt like a nomad who had traveled far from home and couldn't find my way back.

That morning, God seemed farther away than ever. To be honest, my spirit was thirsty, and my faith felt shallow. I could identify with all those people who had written about their souls feeling like "a barren desert." I closed and locked the door of my office, not sure if I could go on in my ministry. I was dying for a new awareness and the real touch of God in my life.

As I prayed that morning and admitted my own failures to share the truth of God's love and possess it in my heart, I remembered a Native American saying I had once heard growing up in Oklahoma. The wisdom of the proverb was profound to me in that moment of spiritual despair: "The longest journey you will make in your life is the journey from your head to your heart." The distance between my mind and my soul felt very real to me that day. I considered all the knowledge I possessed about Jesus, and yet I was not experiencing the intimate presence of my loving Savior on a heart level. That morning was a turning point in my life. There in the quiet and the stillness behind my locked office door, I invited Christ to show up . . . and He certainly did.

That moment began a journey where God helped me recognize that none of my theological training had prepared me to answer the spiritual dilemma I was facing. You see, all my degrees and my seminary studies attempted to resolve my spiritual struggles through biblical thinking, systematic belief structures, and rational thought. While I recognized the importance of those things, I had wrongly assumed that study, intellectual awareness, and cognitive knowledge were enough to produce a healthy and connected spiritual life.

I had been trained to think that if I simply worked at applying the Word of God to my life, I would naturally reflect the character of God in my behavior. In other words, if I knew everything I needed to know about the love of God in my head, then I would also feel and experience the presence and love of God in my heart. For years, this approach had made logical sense . . . until the day my heart didn't allow me to believe it anymore. Mercifully, God brought me to that very moment of desperation when I finally understood I needed to change.

My friend, it became apparent to me that I had left my heart out of the equation. I began to see that I was incapable of thinking my way into a relationship with Christ. I realized the abundant God-centered life required focusing my heart on Christ and spending time being mindful of His presence. I also realized that my dilemma and its solution weren't anything new. They had been written about and practiced since the days of the early church. I simply had to go back and learn from many of the influential men and women who had shaped the Christian faith.

As I was a longtime Christian and a pastor, my intellectual faith was, of course, very genuine. But I found that I desperately needed to create intentional space to experience the love of God in my heart each day. I began to study and explore and pray about how God's love could transcend my intellect and being. My spiritual transformation started with the same questions that maybe you are asking yourself today: *Why do my thoughts and feelings constantly wander from the love of Jesus and the intimacy with Him that I so desire? How can I keep my heart open to Christ in such a fast-talking and faster-moving world? How can I nurture and maintain daily intimacy with God in the hectic pace of modern life?*

For me, the journey was a matter of survival. I knew I did not need to learn or study anything more about God; what I was thirsty for was a deeper connection. I needed to know an intimate relationship with Christ in my heart. All the standard answers from my training seemed insufficient for producing that kind of spiritual life. I realized that I needed to discover how to be mindful of God in a mindless world. I wanted to learn to live in the fullness of the moment and be truly alive in Christ.

That morning, with Christ present in the quiet of my office, was the first step toward learning the discipline of simply sitting in His presence. Day by day, I learned to quiet my busy mind and release all the worldly thoughts and anxieties that kept me from communing with God. I learned how to invite

His presence into the stillness of my life. I discovered how to find Him in the quiet of my soul, even with the chaos of the world swirling around me. I explored my heart and found the indwelling presence of the Spirit of God. Frankly, I had to set aside many of the theological prejudices from my evangelical life in order to discover the gift of living in harmony and unity with God.

Through Christ's leading, I rediscovered the teaching and examples of the Desert Fathers and Mothers who practiced solitude and silence beginning in the third and fourth centuries. I learned through their direction how to experience inner peace and the presence of God. I learned to meditate and use the "Jesus Prayer"—"Lord Jesus Christ, Son of God, have mercy on me a sinner"—based on Luke 18:13, in order to anchor my full attention upon Christ.

I also read *Practicing the Presence of God*, the collection of writings by Brother Lawrence, a seventeenth-century French lay monk, and I discovered that being mindful wasn't new to our faith. I also learned that Protestants had used the term *watchfulness* as a way of focusing their awareness upon Christ. All these forgotten practices seemed so relevant to modern life. I learned to calm my thoughts and to meditate on God's presence using the Psalms. I learned to become still in my spirit like Jesus when He stole away from His disciples and spent time alone with His Father. Most of all, I learned that all these rich spiritual practices were everywhere in Christian tradition.

I am not exaggerating when I say my life was transformed on this journey of discovering what many call contemplative faith practices. I found that there is a divine mystery in the quiet when I am alone with God. I was overjoyed to discover a depth of love and peace in my heart that is indescribable and eternal.

In my relationship with God, an essential truth regarding time became very apparent. I learned that I can only "be" present with God in the now or the present moment. Over time, I learned how to practice *living* in the present moment with God. It wasn't overnight. It was a discipline that took repetition. But the concept of being present with God revolutionized my life, my faith, my relationships, and my ministry. Once I found that the intimate presence of God was always there for me, I was wrapped up in a holy embrace of mercy, grace, and love.

Since it was such a transformation, I set out to share my experience with a few close friends. I quickly found that my desperation for intimacy with God amidst the noise and pressures of modern-day life was a common dilemma. Before long, I had connected with a million people from all backgrounds and all walks of life who also wanted to journey into a more grounded and mindful relationship with Christ. That journey was the inspiration for the book you now hold in your hands. I sincerely hope that these daily readings will open your heart and take you on the same healing journey that I have experienced.

In the Presence of Jesus is a forty-day contemplative experience meant to help you become fully aware of the living, resurrected Jesus. It is designed to ground you in the presence of Christ and introduce you to the important contemplative ideas that have been forgotten in many of our Christian faith traditions. I encourage you to open these pages and create space in your life to anticipate God's arrival. I pray that no matter where you are on your life journey, you will find a secret place in His presence that you never dreamed existed. I want to invite you to listen for the voice of God in the silence of your heart.

My hope is that, during these coming weeks, you will discover practices that will help you let go of your thoughts and exchange them for the thoughts and feelings of God. I believe you will find the hidden treasure your spirit has been longing for as you learn to invite the presence of Christ into your life, just as I did. I know you will find that God's presence is always here, surrounding you and dwelling within you. After all, He tells us that He stands at our door and knocks, patiently waiting on us to answer (Revelation 3:20). May you find Christ, who is eternally longing for you to turn to Him, always healing you, forever teaching you, and steadfastly fulfilling His promises to you.

Blessings in Christ,
Pastor Paul

Entering the Seasons
of the Great "I Am"

How to Use This Forty-Day Devotional

This devotional actually began in the most natural of ways, with an unexpected friendship and an organic conversation over coffee, as Pastor Paul and I connected in our mutual battle to stay spiritually grounded despite the chaos of modern-day life. Our shared interest in contemplative Christian disciplines led us to create a daily exercise that could help us maintain our connection to God. This devotional is a resource spiritually rooted in historical faith practices that the church has simply lost touch with over the years. Today, we need these practices more than ever. To put it in the words of the Native American proverb that changed everything for my friend Paul, we hope that this devotional will help you connect your head to your heart.

In a Richard Foster book from the 1970s, I noticed a reference to the noise and hurry of modern life that works to separate us from our awareness of the Divine. It is astounding to consider how much truer that is today. I'm sure you've noticed the insidious way modern life—with its digital universes attached to our hands and wrists, and instantaneous connections fixed in our ears—can uproot our faith by keeping us fixated on *anything* but the present moment. I've even read that in the not-too-distant future, connectability somehow could be integrated into our bodies! All this has led us into an age where our levels of anxiety, fear, loneliness, and depression continue to soar.

Fortunately, a great antidote for this deep unrest can be found—not in some new device, pill, or high-minded formula but in a daily spiritual routine. It is an ancient and straightforward practice used by Christian believers for more than a thousand years. And it is actually quite simple. We believe spending time intentionally focused on the presence of God can place you on solid ground. But you must embrace being present and mindful. Learning to practice the awareness of God, to enter the presence of the Great "I Am," to sit in stillness with Jesus each day, is the only real way to find peace in the world. It is truly how God transforms us. We hope this book can help lead you into the arms of Jesus moment by moment. So let's begin by answering some questions that will help you get the most from this forty-day experience.

Why Is the Book Organized into Four Movements Called Seasons?

The four movements of the devotional are called seasons because so many of Jesus' parables used agricultural references. Most of us have lost the truth of how valuable slow and natural growth is. In our instant download, on-demand, fast-food culture, we've lost our connection to the healthy rhythms of

God's creation and a life centered on the different seasons of growing and harvesting. Seasons also remind us God is *always* at work, even when we cannot see what He is doing. Spring brings rebirth and new hope. Summer produces growth. Fall releases and celebrates the harvest. Winter is the time of darkness and death, rest and reset. Seasons mirror the cycles we experience in life, cycles of physically growing, raising families, building careers, and relishing retirement. You see, Christ is present and at work through every season of life just as He is through each season of nature. This journey is intended to be a tool to help you grow deep roots in the rich soil of your faith that can sustain you through every season.

How Do the Different Seasons of the Great "I Am" Work Together?

The Gospel of John reminds us that Jesus was there at the beginning of Creation. Entering the presence of the Great "I Am" means that we are bringing our awareness of Christ's presence with us in every moment. Each season of the devotional is designed to wake us to the character of Christ and the way He is present and working in our lives. Every season is organized into a *ten-day movement* that provides us enough time to focus on a particular aspect of God's presence and truly allow it to transform the way we live.

Throughout the Bible, we witness God's people undergoing forty days of waiting: Noah in the ark, Moses on Mount Sinai, Elijah fasting in the desert, and Jesus fasting and being tempted in preparation for His ministry. And throughout the history of Judeo-Christian traditions, forty-day liturgical observances such as Lent have been the measure for spiritual revival, rejuvenation, and regrowth. Our hope is that the next forty days will be transformative for you.

What Will I Learn about Christ in Each Season?

Season One: I Am Always Waiting focuses on building our foundational awareness of the reality that no matter where we are in our lives, Christ is always there for us. It is the bedrock of faith that He is always pursuing us and His grace is always sufficient. This season allows us to explore the compassion and love of Christ, who secured our reconciliation and awaits our homecoming with open arms.

Once we grow in our understanding of God's patience and grace, we move into *Season Two: I Am the Great Physician*, which focuses on opening our hearts to the truth that Christ is always our cure. Not just for our physical ailments but also for our emotional and spiritual brokenness. Christ invites us to bring all our sins, our illnesses, and our wounds to Him for healing. He longs to make us whole.

In *Season Three: I Am the Way*, we progress into meditating on the eternal reality that Christ is our Teacher—He is always instructing us, leading us to follow in His footsteps, and working to perfect us. He is shaping us in His image. And if we follow in His footsteps, we will find eternal joy.

Season Four: I Am the Promise is the culmination of accepting Jesus' goodness. We spend the final ten days building our trust in God. No matter what we face in life, no matter what season we are in, we serve a God who is always "for us." This season is a movement into meditating on and accepting the truth that Jesus is always our Advocate and His promises to us endure forever. He is always fighting for us, longing for us, defending us, and wanting the best for us!

Daily Application: How Do I Use the Book?

Each day's reading and practice are designed to take approximately ten to fifteen minutes. Try to find a quiet space where you won't be interrupted, preferably in the morning! This was quite challenging for me. I had to retreat to corners of my house and even my back porch early in the morning to find quiet. You might want to use a journal for the reflection activities or to write down your thoughts each day, but you certainly don't have to. Paul and I have found the reflection activities make for some great small group discussions if you choose to go on this journey with a community. There are many parts of this book intended to introduce you to contemplative faith practices, but it can also be used as a straightforward devotional.

What Is the Invocation?

Invocation is just a fancy word for inviting Christ's presence into your devotional time. The invocation is designed to be a short prayer of invitation. For several moments, you can repeat the invocation while focusing on your breath. This prayer can help bring your attention to Jesus and your awareness to the present moment. This is an age-old Christian practice that is often called the "Centering Prayer" or the "Prayer of the Heart."

At the beginning of each season, we provide you with a unique approach to using the invocation as a spiritual exercise by reading each line and allowing it to bring you into the presence of Christ or into the Holy Now. Feel free to try the traditional contemplative approach or just prayerfully use the sentence to invite the Holy Spirit into your time of devotion. The invocation is the same for the entire ten-day season so that you can grow accustomed to using the same words. On some days, my thoughts are like kites in a strong breeze, and no matter how hard I try to focus on God's presence, I keep thinking of meetings later in the day or my children or some nagging work issue. Other days, I am able to focus immediately. Don't be discouraged if you find this challenging at first. And remember, as Scripture promises, whenever you invite the Great "I Am" into your space, He will make His enduring presence known.

How Do I Use the Time with Jesus?

Each day begins with a personal note as if it were written by Jesus to you. It has been drawn carefully from the accompanying Scriptures and communicates biblically researched and theologically grounded truths about God's enduring presence and nature. It is meant to open your heart to the voice of Jesus. Each of the forty daily notes is designed to point you toward the eternal truths of Jesus' grace, love, and desire to connect with you. It is important to understand that each of them contains a lesson teaching a biblical truth that will help you grow deeper roots into the understanding of Christ's character. You may find some notes are more meaningful to you than others. You will also discover as you reread and reuse this book that they will likely mean different things to you as your circumstances change and you move through seasons of your life journey. We know from experience that God can use these to speak specifically into a situation you may be facing in your life this very day.

How Do I Use the Scripture?

Each daily reading includes several Scripture verses that support the truth of Christ's character as it relates to you. You may want to read them slowly and prayerfully several times, asking God to reveal Himself through His Word. Meditating on Scripture in this way is an introduction to an ancient Christian practice called *Lectio Divina*. On some days, you may even feel led to write out a verse and put it in a place where you will see it often. Praying a Scripture over and over is a great practice. Of course, the traditional approach of memorizing each Bible verse that speaks truth and hope to you can also be an incredible life-giving discipline.

What Is the Purpose of the Reflection?

This section of the daily reading challenges you to apply the spiritual lessons and biblical truths to the context of your daily life and your ongoing journey with Jesus. It also helps you move toward a deeper understanding of the Great "I Am" and His enduring love for you. You may want to keep a journal and write your responses to the daily reflection activities. The reflection can also be used as a great catalyst for community discussion if you are journeying through the forty days with a small group. At the very least, the reflection will provide some challenges for you to consider and some practices to apply to your life.

How Can I Implement the Daily Prayer?

The prayer is a directive that asks Jesus to continue to show Himself to you throughout your day. It reinforces the daily practice of coming before God and depending on Him to guide you. Each prayer highlights the truths of God's presence in your life. Not only does God respond to our prayers, but He changes our hearts as we learn to pray faithfully. We sincerely hope that this formal prayer practice grows into a daylong, informal, running conversation with Jesus. I have found it helpful not just to begin each morning with a formal prayer like this but to come back to this prayer at the end of my day as well.

What Should I Do with Today's Blessing?

The blessing is the benediction of your daily devotion. It is a challenge for the day. It is also your hope for the day. In a small group setting, it should be read aloud together. I have found reading the blessing out loud, even when I am working through the devotional time in solitude, seems to set the tone for the rest of my day. You are declaring to the world that your hours ahead are committed to your Creator. It is the final affirmation that God is not just present with you in these few moments, but that He is on the move with you wherever you go. We have found that it is often helpful to write this blessing down and repeat it throughout the day.

Some Final Thoughts

Let me assure you that anyone can use this book! In fact, it is designed for people who have no experience with contemplative faith practices at all. It is okay if you have never even heard words such as *contemplative*, *prayer of the heart*, or *mindfulness*. (Although we do think those of you who already use these ancient Christian practices will enjoy it as well.) We wrote this book with the simple mission of helping you grow deep and unshakable roots that stretch into the well of Living Water that is Christ's very presence. And we know that those roots can hold you steady in the chaos of modern life, as they have for us. I want to encourage you to take the parts of the reading that you find helpful to connect you to the presence of Christ and simply leave the rest. Above all, may you discover the peace of the resurrected Jesus in new and redeeming ways through these pages.

With grace and gratitude,
Matt Litton

I Am Always Waiting

The Centering Prayer

Dear Jesus, may I be *still* and *aware* that Your
enduring love is always present and waiting on me.

Dear Jesus, may I be *still* and *aware* that Your
enduring love is always present.

Dear Jesus, may I be *still* and *aware*
of Your enduring love.

Dear Jesus, may I be *still* and *aware*.

Dear Jesus, may I be *still*.

Dear Jesus, may I *be*.

I AM ALWAYS
AT YOUR DOOR

INVOCATION
Dear Jesus, may I be *still* and *aware* that Your enduring
love is always present and waiting on me.

Listen up! I stand at your door and knock. And I promise
that in every moment of your life, I am *present* and *patiently*
waiting to commune with you. Since the beginning of time,
My eternal blueprint and My deepest desire has been to
walk closely with you through every step and every season
of your life. Why? Because I want to reveal My love to you,
to share My grace with you, and because I never want you
to feel alone or hopeless. But you should also know that I
will not kick your door down. I will never force My way into
your life.

I understand how crazy your living space can feel behind
your closed door. I know about the restless thoughts that

keep you awake at night. I recognize the anxiety you feel for your loved ones and how often those worries invade your entire being. I know that you feel you have so much to do and so little time to do it. I hear you when you wonder if you will ever get a moment's peace. I know how loud and over-powering life's uncertainties can seem as they swirl around you. But even when you are too distracted or overwhelmed to hear Me, I am still here, calling your name.

And when you are ready to let Me in, you simply need to open the door, and I will be standing there. You do not have to clean house or prepare dinner for Me. You don't have to dress up or try to put your best foot forward. You don't have to worry about where you have been or what you have done when you invite Me in. Leave all those worries to Me. I just want to be with you. When you invite My presence into your life, peace, comfort, and abiding joy will rush into the depths of your soul. My work of true salvation begins when you encounter My love and ask Me to reside in your heart. I cannot wait to dwell with you and be a part of every aspect of your life.

Remember that I Am the Creator of all the stars in the sky. I Am the Author of time. I Am the Alpha and Omega, and yet I have come to stand at *your* door because My deepest desire is for us to be together. I am always patient and stead-fast in anticipation of your invitation. I am forever longing to share My love with you. I want to move into your life so that you can witness My resurrected glory the way the apostle Paul did. This very day, this very moment, in this very breath, even in the most chaotic moments of your life, I stand at your door and knock. Are you ready to welcome Me?

SCRIPTURE

Look! I stand at the door and knock. If you hear my voice
and open the door, I will come in, and we will share a meal
together as friends.

REVELATION 3:20

Be . . . as though you were waiting for your master to
return from the wedding feast. Then you will be ready to
open the door and let him in the moment he arrives and
knocks.

LUKE 12:35-36

REFLECTION

There is something invasive about even a loved one coming
into the intimacy of your home. It can be extremely stressful
to try to get your house perfect before someone visits. But
consider the profound revelation that the God of the universe
did not wait for you to come to Him, but He patiently waits
outside your door. The truth is that Jesus longs to be invited
into every moment of your life, whether you are experiencing
stress, worry, grief, or joy. He wants to bring His presence and
unconditional love to every aspect of your existence. As you
go through the busyness of this day, quiet yourself to listen
for Jesus' gentle knock. Consider what anxiety, need, relationship, and moment He is patiently waiting for you to release
to Him. What areas of your life are you trying to keep hidden
from Christ?

DAILY PRAYER

Lord Jesus, please help me hear Your gentle knock today. Clear my mind of anything that distracts me from responding and inviting You in. Thank You for patiently waiting. I will let go of the illusion that I need to do anything to get my life in order before I open myself to You. I invite You into the living spaces of my life this very moment. Forgive me for shutting You out. Fill my life with Your Spirit, and bring me the deep and abiding joy that You have promised. Amen.

TODAY'S BLESSING

May you boldly invite the God of the universe into the living spaces of your life today. May you sit in silence as He moves throughout each room of your life. And no matter where you go, may you always be aware that He gently knocks at your door.

TWO

BE STILL AND KNOW THAT I AM

INVOCATION
Dear Jesus, may I be *still* and *aware* that Your enduring love is always present and waiting on me.

My child, you have been living on the run for a long time. If you just stop to consider how you spend your days, you will see that underneath your activities, consumption, and constant hurrying hides a deep longing for fulfillment and meaning. All your accomplishments, the money you earn, the places you travel to, and your endless lists to check off will only leave you feeling empty at the end of the day. You rush through life because you are afraid you'll miss out on something. You race to one destination and then are compelled to hurry to the next place. Yet none of your activities, achievements, acquisitions, or new experiences will ever bring you what you are truly seeking. So much of your life is consumed with the exhausting and desperate search for joy.

I understand that your self-worth is wrapped up in what you believe you can accomplish. Unfortunately, time does not stand still as you chase after all these dreams. Your life is like a vapor. Only I can give you what you are truly longing for. And I know that living as you are will burn you out and leave you feeling empty. Without My strength and rest, your heart will fail beneath the strain of this desperate search. I want you to stop what you are doing today and breathe in My presence. I want you to ask yourself what you are really running from. Where exactly do you think you are going?

This very day, I want you to simply be still and know Me.

Be still and know that only I can satisfy the deep hunger in your heart. Be still and know that only I Am the truest and deepest source of joy. Stop all your incessant activity and acknowledge that My presence is the only place where you can find peace for your restless soul. You see, when you finally stand still to listen, you will hear My voice calling you into joy and fulfillment.

When you stop and simply turn your face to seek My Kingdom, you will discover there was no need for you to do anything except enjoy My presence and *be* who I created you to be. Be still now and know. Be still and know that I Am the source of all you have been looking for your entire life. Be still this day and know that I Am.

SCRIPTURE

Be still, and know that I am God! I will be honored by every nation. I will be honored throughout the world.

PSALM 46:10

Seek the Kingdom of God above all else, and live righteously, and he will give you everything you need.

MATTHEW 6:33

REFLECTION

We spend so much of our lives running here and there in an effort to achieve, to excel, to impress, to find that elusive fulfillment we desire. Yet we know the answer is not found in what we can do because the truth is written on our hearts. Everlasting joy and fulfillment have nothing to do with our efforts and our incessant running. In fact, all we need to do is stand still and be. Are you struggling to be still and know God? Today, consider all the ways you are still pursuing joy and hoping to achieve fulfillment under your own power. What do you need to let go of in your life to simply be still in the presence of Jesus?

DAILY PRAYER

Lord Jesus, thank You for loving me before I loved You. Please show me the ways that I am trying to find joy and fulfillment apart from You. Please calm my restless soul and help me be still. Allow me to know in the deepest parts of my being that I am loved by You, that who I am in You is what matters. Help me to be still and know that You are God. To be still and know that You are the I Am. To be still and know. To be still. To be. Amen.

TODAY'S BLESSING

May you surrender all the ways that you are trying to find joy
and fulfillment on your own. May you be still this day and
know that Jesus is the source of everything you desire. May
you find stillness and peace in the very moments you need
His presence the most.

THREE

I AM PRESENT IN THE QUIET OF THE GARDEN

INVOCATION
Dear Jesus, may I be *still* and *aware* that Your enduring
love is always present and waiting on me.

Today, I want to remind you of your *truest* story. I want you
to remember what it really means to be human. You see, at
the beginning of the world, we walked and talked together
during the cool of the day. In the silence of the Garden of
Eden, we simply relished each other's company. And you were
beginning to discover the joy of living and to recognize the
goodness of the natural world all around you. Everything that
was Mine was truly yours, and none of your needs would ever
go unmet.

But then, you chose to stop trusting Me to care for you.
When I came to talk, you ran away and hid from Me. You
became consumed with what you thought was best for you,
what you needed to own or accomplish, how you needed to

look or talk, what you needed to kill or conquer in order to find joy and fulfillment. And then, as the years went by, you filled your world with just enough noise to distract you from My voice. You created a distance between us that broke My heart.

Let Me remind you about the Story that is so much greater than your choice to go and hide from Me in your sin and shame. Since the very moment that you decided on this great estrangement, I began working to bring your heart back to Me. From that day, I set in motion My divine conspiracy to return you to the silence and intimacy of our walks together in Eden. I have longed for you to once again rest in My love.

It is now time for you to let go of all the things you have used to separate us. I challenge you this day to truly understand that I have already forgiven you for everything. When you ran from My love, I chased after you all the way to the cross. I sacrificed everything so that we could be together again. Remember My words? "It is finished!"

The only thing that can keep you from My love is you, but you will have to work very hard to avoid My loving reach. I long for you to rediscover how deeply I want to be with you and once again trust that I am better than anything this world has to offer you. I want you to remember how we lived in joyful communion in the sanctuary of Eden, before the world of artificial noise and chaos distracted you. My creation was good. Your life was good. You were good.

My deepest desire is to restore that heart-to-heart connection between us. I want you to intimately experience Me, moment by moment, in the goodness of the Holy Now. Yes, I can make you good again. And so, My child, come to Me this very moment to rediscover the quiet of the Garden, where your heart is no longer separated from My presence . . . where you can once again hear My voice.

SCRIPTURE

Then God said, "Let us make human beings in our image, to be like us." . . . So God created human beings in his own image. In the image of God he created them; male and female he created them. Then God blessed them.

GENESIS 1:26-28

Then the man and his wife heard the sound of the LORD God as he was walking in the garden in the cool of the day, and they hid from the LORD God among the trees of the garden.

GENESIS 3:8, NIV

REFLECTION

The Creator of the universe wants to come to you in silence. The first pages of the Bible remind you of what it truly means to be human. You were created to live in communion with God and walk with Him daily. Yes, you may have made sinful choices in your life, just like Adam and Eve, causing you to be separated from God. But remember that the Bible is the Love Story of how God is eternally pursuing you. He desires the same intimacy you once experienced together in the Garden. Today, this very moment, God wants you to stop hiding in shame. He asks you to stop covering up your pain with the noise of the world. He is waiting for you to find Him in the silence. He will be there with you. What has made you run from Him? Where can you find the silence of His presence in your life today? Where can you go to hear Christ's voice calling to you?

DAILY PRAYER

Lord Jesus, walk with me today in the silence of the Garden and help me hear Your voice. Forgive me for not fully trusting You and for disobeying You time and time again. Reassure me of Your unconditional love and forgiveness in the moments that I want to hide from You. Help me to find joy and contentment in Your presence. Amen.

TODAY'S BLESSING

May Jesus remind you that your deepest purpose is to commune with Him. May you know He delights in simply walking with you throughout the day. May you hear His voice calling you back to the silence of the Garden.

FOUR

I AM THE GOOD KING

INVOCATION
Dear Jesus, may I be *still* and *aware* that Your enduring
love is always present and waiting on me.

I Am your good King. I know that the word *king* has prob-
ably lost much of its meaning to you. Yet the modern world
is still full of kings who rule under different names. Just look
around you: They are the dictators, prime ministers, presi-
dents, politicians, CEOs, superintendents, and authority figures who affect your life. Some of them you chose and some
of them you didn't. And some of the kings in your world
aren't actual people; they may just be the dreams and desires
you have put before Me as idols in your life. No matter what
form they take, often these earthly kings are simply *not* good.

I Am the only good King.

Maybe you have been mistreated by one of these authority
figures. I assure you that while they may be able to hurt you,

they have no true power over your heart and your mind. They cannot harm your eternal soul. In this very moment, I want you to know that there is no one in heaven or earth over whom I do not have complete power. Yes, you are My child, and I love you just as a parent loves a son or a daughter, but I am also a heavenly King, and I desire to rule your life completely.

My Kingdom is not built on rules, regulations, and retributions like your earthly kingdoms. I have crafted the foundation of My Kingdom with everlasting peace and joy. My rule is always just. My judgment is always fair. And the great influence and power of My Kingdom are found not in coercion or brute force but in the sacrificial and invitational love of My death on the cross . . . a choice I made because of My love for you.

Even though I oversee every detail of this universe, I still desire you to participate in My Kingdom. I invite you to accept My Kingship and My loving rule. Why? Because you have an important role to play in restoring My divine love and order to the world. You see, you have been placed right where you are this day to reflect My power and good governance over all creation and to participate in bringing My love to others.

Accepting me as your true King means that you must give up control of your life. You have spent so much time operating as though you are king or believing that the authorities of this world are kings of your life. Chaos, anxiety, hatred, and fear are all clear signs that you are being ruled by someone or something other than Me. The more you resist My Kingship, the greater the unrest and uncertainty you will feel.

But accepting Me as your King is your choice. It will always be your choice.

In the depths of your heart, you know that I love you beyond measure; open your heart and trust Me to rule over you. Seek My Kingdom, and I will take care of all your needs. I'll take your worry away. Open your heart and trust Me to be your good King. Let My presence fill your heart with reassurance and peace this day.

SCRIPTURE

"For I know the plans I have for you," says the LORD. "They are plans for good and not for disaster, to give you a future and a hope."

JEREMIAH 29:11

Don't copy the behavior and customs of this world, but let God transform you into a new person by changing the way you think. Then you will learn to know God's will for you, which is good and pleasing and perfect.

ROMANS 12:2

REFLECTION

Consider the people who wield power over aspects of your life. Have you ever been mistreated by someone with authority over you? How did it feel? Jesus is King and wants to have authority over you. Do you trust Him with that complete authority? In what ways do you try to maintain control over your own life? Write down areas or situations in your life in which you need to acknowledge and trust God as King and ruler. Spend a few moments considering what it means for God to be not just a good Father but your good King.

DAILY PRAYER

Lord Jesus, help me to embrace Your rule over every area of my life. Show me the ways You already are the good King in my world. I want to represent Your Kingship at work, in my family, and with my neighbors, but I need Your guidance. Please help me submit to Your authority in all that I do. Amen.

TODAY'S BLESSING

May you bend your knee this day to the King of Kings, to the Prince of Peace, to Christ, who rules over the universe and desires to rule over your heart. May you accept His invitation to submit to His rule today and experience the benefits that await you in His Kingdom, especially His gifts of peace and love.

FIVE

I AM YOUR PERFECT FRIEND

INVOCATION

Dear Jesus, may I be *still* and *aware* that Your enduring love is always present and waiting on me.

What do you look for in a friend? Is it loyalty? Trustworthiness? Empathy? Accountability? How many people in your life would you consider to be close friends? I know that even the most faithful friends may come and go through the many seasons of your life. But I will never leave you—even when you don't feel My presence. I will never turn My back on you—even when you turn your back on Me. I don't keep score of your rights and wrongs. Think about the loyalty of your most faithful and loving friends, and know that I have put them in your life as special gifts to be a small reflection of My desire to be your friend. My Father was called a friend of Abraham and Moses in the great Story of love. And just as I called My faithful followers My friends, I want you to understand that I willingly went to the ultimate length to be your closest and ever-present companion.

This may be big news to you today! Maybe you have never even imagined the idea of a God who also wants to be your friend. But it is true. In fact, I long for a deep friendship with you that has no limits. As your friend, I promise you that everything that My Father has given Me is yours too. As your friend, I invite you to talk to Me about anything, at any time. As your friend, I *always* enjoy your company. I will never tire of spending time with you. I will never grow weary of hearing your voice.

When your earthly friends leave you and go back to their own lives before the sun sets, I am the One who stays with you through the darkest of nights. I Am the Friend who remains by your side to celebrate with you in the times of your greatest joy. I am present with you each and every moment of the day. There is no need to ever worry or be afraid or feel alone. I Am the friend who knows your next word before you even say it and who feels your next breath before you even take it. I Am the Friend who will never leave you or forsake you.

Dear one, I want you to turn your eyes upon Me and look into My face, and allow all the things of this earth to grow dim. So do not fear, for I am always close; do not be dismayed, for I am always your friend. I will strengthen you and help you; I will hold you up when you need it most. I want nothing more than to enjoy your company, to share your triumphs and defeats, to hear your laughter and to dry your tears. Open your heart to Me, and I will be your perfect Friend.

SCRIPTURE

You are my friends if you do what I command.

JOHN 15:14

No longer do I call you servants, for the servant does not know what his master is doing; but I have called you friends, for all that I have heard from my Father I have made known to you.

JOHN 15:15, ESV

And so it happened just as the Scriptures say: "Abraham believed God, and God counted him as righteous because of his faith." He was even called the friend of God.

JAMES 2:23

REFLECTION

No friend is faultless or perfect, and yet friendships can be such an incredible gift in your life. Think of the ways in which friendships have made your life better through love, laughter, and encouragement. When you think of Jesus, do you most often consider Him a King or a Father? The Bible tells us He is also a Friend. Think of your heartfelt conversations with close friends. Do you talk to Christ in that way? Do you make time with Jesus a priority just as you do with your personal friends? How might this new understanding of Christ as your perfect Friend help you today?

DAILY PRAYER

Lord Jesus, help me embrace Your presence as a close Friend. Today, open my heart to the truth that I can reveal anything to You—my frustrations and contentment, my failures and successes, my doubts and insights. You are keenly interested in everything about me. May I know Your unconditional friendship not only in my most difficult and lonely moments but in my most joyous moments too. Amen.

TODAY'S BLESSING

May you revel in the presence of a Savior who is the closest and most accessible Friend you could ever have. May His divine company encourage and uplift you. May your day be filled with the joy of knowing you are never alone.

SIX

I AM THE TENDERNESS OF A MOTHER'S LOVE

INVOCATION
Dear Jesus, may I be *still* and *aware* that Your enduring
love is always present and waiting on me.

My dearest child, I know that sometimes it feels impossible
for you to comprehend how much I love you. I long to hold
you with the tenderness of a mother's love. Maybe in the
midst of this world's brokenness, you never knew the care of
a mother. Or perhaps you have heard voices in the religious
crowd explain how you need to show Me your love *before* I
can love you. Maybe you have been taught My love is condi-
tional. I want you to know in the deepest parts of your heart
that nothing could be further from the truth.

There are few things in creation that compare to a mother's unconditional love for her children. Consider a helpless
child. Does she have to earn being swaddled, held close, and

shielded from the cold by her mother? Does a hungry new-born have to do something in order to merit being nursed? When a toddler falls and starts crying, does a mother hesitate to give the child immediate and attentive care? Of course not! Shelter, protection, and nurturing flow from the tenderness freely given from the depths of a mother's heart.

My beloved, in these moments, I ask you to set aside all your past experiences, all that you think you know, and take a moment to observe the deep instincts of motherhood I have embedded throughout creation. Watch the mother bird's instinct to gather worms for her young. Think of how the lioness nurses her cubs, then instructs them in how to find food. You see, even the natural world is simply a mirror showing My deepest desire to look after and care for you.

I love you with that same fierce tenderness.

I know the depth of a mother's love because My own mother was there for Me. She protected Me from the cold in a Bethlehem manger, and yes, she was there for Me that fateful day at Golgotha. She wept for me at the foot of the cross when I cried out in pain to my heavenly Father and began my journey to bring you into My loving arms. Such is the depth of My care for you and My compassion for all humankind.

Right now, I want you to take the list you keep of your shortcomings, your failures, and your inadequacies, and give it to Me. I want you to visualize the profound love and affection a mother shows when she cradles her newborn. Allow Me to hold you close in the same way. Trust Me with all your needs.

In My eyes, you are like that newborn who does nothing to earn the tenderness and love of a mother. Once you have accepted that truth, you can learn to love others with the same depth and tenderness as My love for you.

SCRIPTURE

Can a mother forget her nursing child? Can she feel no love for the child she has borne? But even if that were possible, I would not forget you!

ISAIAH 49:15

See how very much our Father loves us, for he calls us his children, and that is what we are!

1 JOHN 3:1

REFLECTION

There are few things in the world like a mother's attentiveness to an infant. Jesus demonstrates the same unconditional tenderness toward you. Just as a mother loves her baby, God freely offers His love to you. Today, think of examples of motherly instincts you see in the world around you. Consider how Mary cared for Jesus from infancy to the cross. In a culture that speaks so often about the masculine qualities of God, how helpful is it to consider that God's tender, motherly love is reflected throughout creation? How does this increase your understanding of God? Spend time considering the ways you try to earn God's love when He is simply wanting to embrace you as a mother cradles an infant child. As you spend time dwelling in Jesus' presence, thank Him for His undivided attention and never-ending love.

DAILY PRAYER

Lord Jesus, please help me to accept Your tenderness today. Open my eyes to the truth that You are always there for me, and that there is nothing I must do to earn Your loving care. Please help me to trust You with all my needs just as an infant trusts and rests in the arms of a mother. Amen.

TODAY'S BLESSING

May you lay down the burden of trying to earn God's tenderness in your life. May you go throughout the day looking for ways that Jesus has met your needs just as a mother would with her child. May Christ's unconditional love for you make your love for Him grow even deeper.

SEVEN

MY GOOD KINGDOM IS YOURS

INVOCATION

Dear Jesus, may I be *still* and *aware* that Your enduring love is always present and waiting on me.

I am the source of all-consuming love that summons you into a new reality. I have called you to a different way of living in and seeing the world. My love welcomes you as a holy citizen of My Kingdom. There is no country on the face of this vast earth that compares to Mine. In fact, the very foundation of all creation is built upon My Kingdom. My child, if you only knew the short distance to this Kingdom of freedom from the bondage of this world, it would simply astound you. It is like a treasure hidden in a field.

No matter where you are or how far you have run away, My Kingdom remains close, open to you whenever you choose to return your heart to Me. All you have to do is call

My name. And I want you to know that My destiny for you is to live in intimate union with Me. I do not call to you as a servant or worker; I long for you to walk alongside Me as an heir in My Kingdom.

I invite you to participate in My new reality where the poor are always welcome, the hungry are always well fed at my table, the mourners are held close and comforted, the slaves are freed from oppression, the sick are healed, the tired are given a place to safely rest, the unloved become deeply loved, the merciful and those who work for peace are celebrated above all others. There is no entrance fee or secret handshake for admission. There is no status or background check to get in. Everyone is invited to the party. In fact, there is nothing you have to do to enter My Kingdom except acknowledge Me as your Lord and walk in My footsteps.

Take these visions of My Kingdom and make them the tenets of your new life. Your mission is to help others see Me through your life. Let them know that, in My Kingdom, the heart resides free and unbound from the systems of the world. Be My ambassador starting now.

My Good Kingdom resides in your heart this very moment. With My help, it will extend from your heart into your neighborhood and beyond. This new Kingdom takes shape in My presence. Once you embrace your citizenship, its aspects will spill over into your life and the lives of those all around you. Simply let go of your desire for power, let go of your scorekeeping, stop trying to earn your way into My good graces, and detach yourself from earthly allegiances and worldly possessions. Call My name and allow My love to guide you through the Kingdom gates. Acknowledge that you can trust Me with your life. Crown Me your King! My Good

Kingdom is yours. Come and claim this extraordinary inheritance today.

SCRIPTURE

Seek the Kingdom of God above all else, and live righteously, and he will give you everything you need.

MATTHEW 6:33

Since we are his children, we are his heirs. In fact, together with Christ we are heirs of God's glory. But if we are to share his glory, we must also share his suffering.

ROMANS 8:17

REFLECTION

What does Jesus' Kingdom look like to you? Scripture tells us that Christ was there at the very foundation of the world, and evidence of His Kingdom can be found in all aspects of life and creation. God's Kingdom is as close as your breath. Are you truly able to see yourself as an "heir in God's Kingdom"? How can that idea change your self-perception? Write down how your life goals, values, and aspirations align or need to be aligned with Christ's Kingdom goals. How can considering yourself an heir in the Kingdom change the way you see your life and your neighborhood? Write down what responsibility you have to other people as you learn to embrace being an heir with Christ in God's Kingdom.

DAILY PRAYER

Jesus, please help me to remember that I am an exceptional citizen and heir in Your Kingdom. Give me both a fervent desire and the opportunity to do the work of Your Kingdom in practical ways—caring for the less fortunate, working for peace and justice. Most of all, Jesus, help me to embrace the reality of Your Kingdom in my heart and mind.

TODAY'S BLESSING

May you take on the identity of the Kingdom in which you live. May you remember that you are not only a beloved child of God—you are a coheir with Christ in God's Kingdom. May you experience the peace of His Kingdom today.

EIGHT

I AM WAITING FOR YOUR RETURN TO ME

INVOCATION

Dear Jesus, may I be *still* and *aware* that Your enduring
love is always present and waiting on me.

I told you the story of the younger son who ran away from
home after taking his father's inheritance and then spent all
his money on foolishness. It did not take this wayward son
long before he became so poor and so down and out that he
had no money, nothing to eat, and no place to sleep. This
rebellious son decided on one particularly cold, dark, lonely
night that even his father's hired workers were living much
better than he was. So he swallowed all his pride and returned
home in hopes that he could beg his dad for a job working
the fields as a servant. But the story takes an unexpected twist.
You see, when this estranged father saw his lost son a long
way off on the horizon, he did something that no important

person would ever do in those times. This dad lifted his robe, kicked off his sandals, and ran down the very long driveway of their estate to embrace his disobedient son.

Now, it was commonly known back then that the head of a household would never ever run anywhere. In fact, it would be considered a complete humiliation because, at that time in history, only servants ran. You see, this father's heart was so moved with joy when he saw his son was coming home that he ran as fast as he could to embrace him. Without a second thought about his own dignity, he lowered himself in the eyes of all who witnessed him to run toward the very son who had taken his money and wished him dead.

This very day, My child, I want you to embrace the deep truth in your heart that this great story isn't really about some ancient father and son; it is actually about you and Me. It is about an everlasting love that has no boundaries, keeps no score, and follows no rules. It is about My love for you. You see, it does not matter at all to Me what you have done in your life, where you have been, or even what you have said.

If you will simply turn your feet back in My direction, then just like the father in that ancient story, I will run toward you with no regard for My own dignity and embrace you with joy and grace and complete forgiveness. Just as that father did, I will throw the biggest party in your honor if you will only choose to come home to Me.

Return to Me, and I will give you peace and rest and comfort. I will give you the keys to My house again. I created you with one purpose—to live moment by moment under My care and unfailing love. I will run to rescue you as if you were a lamb that had wandered off the path countless times. Never let the lies of the enemy and the noise of this world keep you from returning to Me. You are My child. My arms are always open, ready to hold you and never let you go.

SCRIPTURE

He made us, and we are his. We are his people, the sheep of his pasture.

PSALM 100:3

So he got up and went to his father. But while he was still a long way off, his father saw him and was filled with compassion for him; he ran to his son, threw his arms around him and kissed him.

LUKE 15:20, NIV

REFLECTION

Consider the many truths about God's love for you found in the story of the Prodigal Son. In those days, for a son to take his father's inheritance and leave the house was the equivalent of wishing the father's death! In that culture, the father was like a king in his home. Still, when the father in Jesus' parable saw his lost son, he ran to meet him! Today, think about the ways you have behaved like a prodigal child. What things have you done that keep you from feeling as if you can spend time in the presence of Christ? List them on a piece of paper. The truth is there is nothing more important to the heavenly Father than embracing you and welcoming you home. There is nothing you can do that will separate you from the love of Christ. Now tear up that list of wrongdoings because your heavenly Father has forgotten it and is too busy running toward you right now!

DAILY PRAYER

Lord Jesus, I admit I can become distracted and wander away, leaving Your protection. Please help me recognize when that happens. Open my eyes to see how much You have sacrificed for me and how much more You want to give. Amen.

TODAY'S BLESSING

May you thank Jesus for never giving up in His relentless pursuit of you, all the way to the cross. There is no place you can disappear—He will always find you. May you surrender to Him anything that is preventing you from returning home. May you experience His reckless and gracious love in every area of your life today.

NINE

I AM FOUND IN THE SACRED SPACE OF SOLITUDE AND SILENCE

INVOCATION

Dear Jesus, may I be *still* and *aware* that Your enduring
love is always present and waiting on me.

Can you hear Me? So many loud and unrelenting voices seek
your attention in today's world. All this manufactured noise
works powerfully to distract you from My faithful presence
and gentle direction. My beloved, these chaotic tones shout
out lies about who you are, what you must do, and what
you need to be considered successful. These voices will leave
you feeling empty and anxious. And yes, there are also well-
intentioned voices present in your life that can often lead you
astray from My deepest desires for you.

This tsunami of information can drown out your awareness of My acceptance and love and make you feel isolated.
But please believe My promise: You are never alone.

There is a sacred space inside you that only opens in

silence and solitude. That is My dwelling place in you, and it holds the keys to the divine healing and rest that you desperately need in your life. I know the pain and brokenness that you carry. Remember that there is nothing you can experience in life that I did not go through. Whenever I needed peace and clarity during My earthly ministry, I retreated to the places where I could be fully present with My Father. Even in the darkest moments, like the night before My crucifixion, I went to a garden for a time of solitude and silence, inviting My Father into My life. I even showed you how to pray and how to find that sacred space.

Come to Me in the stillness and quiet, and I will consecrate that area as holy. You see, your heart needs time away from the world's noise. It needs time to discern My steady voice from other less affirming declarations. That holy quiet can restore your perception of My presence so I can show you what is real and what is not. I can open your eyes to what is life-giving and eternal, as well as what is unimportant and temporal. In solitude and silence, I will expose the lies and the trappings of this world as nothing more than vapor. I will be there to remind you that My love, forgiveness, and guidance are everlasting truths you can depend on.

Meeting Me just as you are in this very moment and in this sacred space will bring you clarity, and I will dispel the dark fears you harbor inside with My light. I will dissolve your illusions of self-preservation, and I will expose the world's lies about your identity. I long for you to hear My voice. Listen for Me, and I will comfort your heart and take away the anxiousness that keeps you up at night. Just as peaceful sleep can bring renewal to your body, My presence will breathe new life into your spirit and fill your soul.

Experience My grace, love, and freedom found in the sacred silence, and I will heal your soul.

SCRIPTURE

He will conceal me there when troubles come; he will hide me in his sanctuary. He will place me out of reach on a high rock.

PSALM 27:5

When you pray, go away by yourself, shut the door behind you, and pray to your Father in private. Then your Father, who sees everything, will reward you.

MATTHEW 6:6

Before daybreak the next morning, Jesus got up and went out to an isolated place to pray.

MARK 1:35

REFLECTION

The world is full of noise and distraction. In fact, most people carry the sound of chaos around in their pockets or bags. We are constantly bombarded with messages on our phones about who we are and what we need to be happy. The world says we have to be connected, and yet this constant connection drowns out the voice of God. Time and time again in Scripture we see Jesus retreating into solitude and silence to connect with His Father. Today, pay particular attention to your schedule. Do you make space for solitude and silence? Are

you afraid to be alone in the quiet? If so, why? Set aside intentional time this week to quietly spend a few minutes listening
for Jesus' voice. He is waiting for you in the silence.

DAILY PRAYER

*Lord Jesus, show Yourself to me this day as I intentionally close
myself off from the noise and connection of the world for these
precious moments to be with You. Make Your peace, Your love,
Your joy, and Your will for me evident in this holy silence. Give
me the resolve, patience, and courage to enter that silence each
day and wait for You. Amen.*

TODAY'S BLESSING

May you continually seek Jesus in the sacred space of silence.
May you find the ever-present joy of Christ in your heart this
day. May He heal you, restore you, and give you the guidance
you need in those quiet moments.

TEN

I AM THE DIVINE PARENT

INVOCATION

Dear Jesus, may I be *still* and *aware* that Your enduring love is always present and waiting on me.

Believe Me when I tell you that you are My dear child. In fact, I have carefully and lovingly crafted you in My image. I chose you long before you even knew of Me. Yes, it is true. I chose you. And I also completely love and accept you just as you are. Even before the very beginning of the world, I could not wait to walk arm in arm with you each day, to hear your voice, to see your smile, and to offer you My embrace. You should know that despite what the world has told you about Me, I am not separated from you by time. I am not speaking to you from some distant place beyond the stars. I am not lost in your yesterdays or in some far-off dreams about tomorrow.

I am here with you right now . . . in this very place, in this very breath, in the Holy Now of this very moment.

I know that in the chaos of life, it can be easy to forget that I am always present and waiting with open arms. I know the world is full of brokenness that can make you feel estranged from Me. Maybe you have been abandoned or hurt by the loved ones in your life. Maybe you have never felt the blessing of unconditional love shown by a parent. Maybe you have never been hugged by a father or mother. My heart breaks for you. But I am here for you. I want you to hear Me say this very day that there is nothing in the universe that can stop Me from loving you, nothing that will keep Me from pursuing a relationship with you. All you need to do is open your heart and recognize My presence at your side this very moment. I can release you from the powers of this broken world and lighten the burdens you carry each day. The power of My love can free you from your fears and doubts about tomorrow.

You are not just a child of this world. You are Mine. You are the child of the Most High King. And as My child, you need never be defined by your failures; be known for your sins and transgressions; or be crippled by your fears. Most important, I will never abandon you, even in the midst of life's biggest messes.

I am here to embrace you when you need it most. I am present to pick you up when you stumble. I am always working to teach and correct you. To gently push you toward the right path. You are no longer defined by anything in this world. You are known and named by Me. And I formed you in your mother's womb to be one of a kind. I have no other child quite like you in all the world. You are the dearest and most valuable of all My creations. Today, I want you to hear the everlasting truth written in the deepest places in all creation: Before you are anything else, you are first and fore-most My beloved child.

SCRIPTURE

You saw me before I was born. Every day of my life was recorded in your book. Every moment was laid out before a single day had passed.

PSALM 139:16

Even before he made the world, God loved us and chose us in Christ to be holy and without fault in his eyes.

EPHESIANS 1:4

REFLECTION

Most parents understand what it means to have a deep love for their children. For those who aren't parents, this same feeling of unconditional love might be lavished on a pet. And yet, even the strongest earthly expressions of love still pale in comparison to the eternal depth of God's boundless love for you. Today, be encouraged by this: You are a beloved child of God—that is your true identity! You are divinely made, one of a kind, more treasured than anything a craftsman could possibly create. Sometimes we lose sight of the truth that there is a God who painstakingly designed us like nothing else in all eternity, whose love for us runs deeper than the love of any parent, who unconditionally longs for us to recognize His divine presence. Take a few moments and consider the ways

God has made you exceptionally unique. Write them down and spend some time in silence asking God to show you the depth of His love.

DAILY PRAYER

Lord Jesus, help me to fully understand that I am Your child. Open my heart to Your abiding presence and allow me to see all the ways You made me unique. Help me to begin to view myself as You see me. Amen.

TODAY'S BLESSING

May you let go of all the ways the world has tried to define you. May you be open to the divine, unconditional love and acceptance of the heavenly Father who meticulously made you for the joy of your companionship. May you embrace your name in these moments: You are the dearest child of the Creator of the universe.

I Am the Great Physician

The Centering Prayer

Dear Jesus, may I be *still* and *aware* of Your healing
power and forgiving love that are present
with me in this Holy Now.

Dear Jesus, may I be *still* and *aware* of Your healing
power and forgiving love that are present.

Dear Jesus, may I be *still* and *aware* of Your healing
power and forgiving love.

Dear Jesus, may I be *still* and *aware*.

Dear Jesus, may I be *still*.

Dear Jesus, may I *be*.

ELEVEN

FIND MY GIFT IN EVERY HARDSHIP

INVOCATION

Dear Jesus, may I be *still* and *aware* of Your healing
power and forgiving love that are present
with me in this Holy Now.

I know the fear and frustration you feel when it seems that
your life is falling apart. It is natural to do everything in your
power to avoid suffering and pain. But in these moments—
when uninvited troubles cause darkness, emptiness, and
abandonment—I want you to listen for My voice. You will
hear My promise in even the most difficult of circumstances.
My child, no matter how hopeless things seem, do not lose
heart. I am always doing a new thing in you. I know these
words may be difficult to hear when you are suffering from
illness, pain, financial difficulties, or broken relationships, but
remember that I am always here with you.

You see, the most difficult circumstances in life are also
when your illusions of self-reliance, independence, and your

way of doing things will crumble beneath your feet. When hardships invade your life, they also break down the walls you have built to separate yourself from My love. And these are the very moments when something new begins. When you must desperately search for firm footing against the wind and storms of life, you will discover that only I can be your strong foundation.

This very day, I want to bring My resurrection power to the hardships you face. In these trying times, I want you to allow Me to clear away everything in your life except for your reliance on Me. I will help you stand upright on My eternal foundation and trust that I will never leave you. I long for you to release the broken dreams, the pain, the illness, and the difficulties you face into My capable hands. I only want your honesty, your emotions, your tears, and your pain—I can handle it all. You see, when you are broken open, I am closer to you than ever. These are the very moments that you will discover what is most important and essential in your life. Let Me build something new with it all!

I invite you to turn and boldly face your difficulties in My name. Do not fear them and do not run from them. Walk hand in hand with Me, and we will uncover the beautiful treasure of My relentless presence underneath it all. This is My great gift to you: a deepening awareness of My unending redeeming love that calls you into a loving unity with all My creation. So sit with Me in prayer and contemplation as you face adversity and circumstances beyond your control. Face your pain and suffering head-on. Walk through them with My strength. Let Me take your brokenness and transform you from the inside out. Trust in Me that, no matter how hopeless it may seem, I will reconcile all things in your life for My

purposes. I will help you find the beautiful gift hidden in
these hardships.

SCRIPTURE

I have told you all this so that you may have peace in me.
Here on earth you will have many trials and sorrows. But take
heart, because I have overcome the world.

JOHN 16:33

He heals the brokenhearted and bandages their wounds.

PSALM 147:3

Rejoice in our confident hope. Be patient in trouble, and keep
on praying.

ROMANS 12:12

REFLECTION

It can be difficult to see anything positive when we are faced
with hardships. But God is often closer than ever in these
moments. What are the things you are facing today that you
do not think you can handle? Are you avoiding difficulties
in your life instead of surrendering them to God? What do
you feel you cannot be honest with God about? What lessons do you think you may learn from the struggles you
are facing? How can you invite Christ into those moments
with you today? Submit to Him. He will renew and transform your perspective as you walk through these challenging

circumstances, and He will help you hear His voice in trying times.

DAILY PRAYER

Lord Jesus, give me the strength this day to face the difficult situations in my life. I surrender these burdens and hardships and ask You to help me carry them. I pray for Your guidance as I navigate these trying times. Break me open and help me to face them head-on. Fill my heart with Your resurrection power through these trials, and change me for Your purposes. Allow me to bring light to those around me who know what I'm going through. Amen.

TODAY'S BLESSING

May your life's difficulties be covered with grace and the knowledge that the risen Savior has already defeated your affliction. May you discover the gift in every hardship. May Christ impart His strength to you today and fill you with great peace and joy.

TWELVE

I AM HEALING YOUR ANGRY SPIRIT

INVOCATION
Dear Jesus, may I be *still* and *aware* of Your healing
power and forgiving love that are present
with me in this Holy Now.

I want to help you confront your anger today. I know you are
holding on to many hurts from your past. Resentment and
anger about these sufferings may feel good in the moment,
and might even provide you with a false sense of protection.
But they will eventually take on a life of their own and will
separate you from what is everlasting and true. Bitterness and
resentment will only distance you from My love. A resentful
and angry spirit will always develop when you are unable to
move past the moments of life that seem unfair and unjust.
My child, I know that these real tragedies and terrible setbacks
are painful, and they can be so hard to release. I know this
because I have felt them too. There is nothing you can experience that I did not go through. Today, I ask you to give those

emotions to Me. Do not hold anything back. I can handle all your hurts.

Remember how the prophet Jonah became resentful when My Father compassionately spared the people who had treated his family so terribly? Consider what might have happened if Joseph had harbored anger toward his brothers who had abandoned him to die in a dark pit. Moses' deep hatred of the Egyptians' cruel treatment of the Israelites actually grew into unspeakable violence. I want you to realize that holding on to anger and bitterness can blind you to My presence.

My child, I have called you to a life of wholeness. I am doing a new work in you that can take the deepest wounds in your life and turn them into your deepest joys. But first you need to realize that nothing good and redemptive can grow in the darkness of anger and bitterness. Pull up those seeds and hand them over to Me! If you allow anger and resentment to take root in your life, you will find yourself becoming suspicious of everyone's motives. You will begin to assume that other people are always out to get you. If resentment is allowed to grow, your heart will become hostile terrain, and you will stop trusting everyone in your life—even Me. You will no longer risk being open and vulnerable.

Jonah soon learned the purpose of My Father's compassion as it was also extended to him. Joseph let go of bitterness and didn't just redeem his own family but rescued an entire nation from starvation. Moses learned to trust My Father and to let Him fight the Israelites' battles, even when things seemed hopeless. And on the cross of Calvary, I bore all the resentment and hate that no one else could endure. I overcame the grave and all the vitriol the world directed at Me, all with you in mind.

So allow Me to heal your anger in these moments. I will

fill your heart with the fruit of My Spirit: love, joy, peace, patience, kindness, goodness, faithfulness, gentleness, and self-control. I will teach you to approach the world with the same openness with which I come to you. I will take your resentment and replace it with the freedom of My compassion and love. Only I can truly heal your spirit.

SCRIPTURE

But the Holy Spirit produces this kind of fruit in our lives: love, joy, peace, patience, kindness, goodness, faithfulness, gentleness, and self-control. There is no law against these things!

GALATIANS 5:22-23

Get rid of all bitterness, rage, anger, harsh words, and slander, as well as all types of evil behavior.

EPHESIANS 4:31

Look after each other so that none of you fails to receive the grace of God. Watch out that no poisonous root of bitterness grows up to trouble you, corrupting many.

HEBREWS 12:15

REFLECTION

So often, the trials and heartaches we face in life can affect our outlook. After we are hurt or injured by others, after so many disappointments, we often begin to see life differently.

The truth is that there is nothing Jesus didn't face and overcome in His earthly ministry. He intimately knows what you are going through. He wants you to surrender your hurts and disappointments to Him before they become ugly. Are you carrying anger and resentment that you need to surrender to Jesus today? How have those feelings hurt other people in your life? Do you need to forgive someone who has hurt you? When you do, Jesus will change your angry attitude to one that reflects His love and compassion.

DAILY PRAYER

Lord Jesus, show me where I have become critical and angry. Forgive me for holding on to hurt and disappointment and allowing them to grow and fester in my life. This day, I take those experiences and lay them at the foot of the cross. I pray that You would transform my anger and resentment into love, joy, peace, patience, kindness, goodness, faithfulness, gentleness, and self-control. Amen.

TODAY'S BLESSING

May you be freed of the burdens and hopelessness that result from a critical and angry spirit. May you lay your hurts at the feet of Jesus today and walk with a lightened heart in the freedom of His grace and love.

THIRTEEN

I AM HEALING
HURTFUL WORDS

INVOCATION

Dear Jesus, may I be *still* and *aware* of Your healing
power and forgiving love that are present
with me in this Holy Now.

My heart breaks for the ways you have been injured by the
hurtful words of others. And I know it can be impossible
at times for you to really hear My words of hope when you
have been so deeply wounded in this way. Words are far more
powerful than anyone truly understands. They can hurt you,
destroy you, discourage you, and leave you in lasting pain. I
know that you are carrying the scars of the cruel or thought-
less words of others.

Despite the rejection you may feel, I want you to hear
Me when I say that I love you and only desire to heal the
injuries you have sustained from these ill-spoken words. I
want you to understand the eternal truth that those who hurt

you with their language do not have the last say. On the Day of Judgment, everyone will be held accountable—not just for their actions but for every word they have spoken. And remember that My words are the only everlasting reality. I Am the very first Word, and I Am the very last Word in all the universe.

My child, because I have the final say, I want you to stop repeating those words that have brought you pain and, instead, listen closely to the words I have spoken to you. I want you to write My words on your heart this day because they are eternal and because they are true. While the words that hurt you will pass away, My words will endure for- ever. Remember that it was the very power of My words that spoke all creation into existence—everything you see around you.

So listen intently to Me: I knew and loved you before you were in your mother's womb. In fact, I chose you before the very foundation of the world. I know the exact number of hairs on your head. I know the struggles you face, and I understand each and every one of your deepest needs.

I was present with you when those hurtful words were spoken to you, and I felt the anguish they caused you. I know the tongue is powerful, and it can offer life-affirming words or destructive ones. My heart was broken by those words because I value you so deeply. My Kingdom is yours. You are true royalty. You are My most precious child. Allow Me to write the words of My eternal love over the pain you feel. I want to redeem your scars from those hurtful words.

Remember that you are never defined by the words of others. Your life is shaped only by My words. Embrace this truth: I came into this fallen and broken world to reveal My love for you. In fact, I loved you so much that I died for you on a cross, and I conquered death when I rose from the grave—just for you. I came to bring forgiveness and healing to the lost and brokenhearted. In this moment, meditate on My words, and I will redeem all those malicious words you have endured. I will replace them with My vocabulary of everlasting hope and grace. Listen closely, and My words will lift you up, encourage you, and heal you this day.

SCRIPTURE

You made all the delicate, inner parts of my body and knit me together in my mother's womb. Thank you for making me so wonderfully complex! Your workmanship is marvelous—how well I know it. You watched me as I was being formed in utter seclusion, as I was woven together in the dark of the womb. You saw me before I was born. Every day of my life was recorded in your book. Every moment was laid out before a single day had passed.

PSALM 139:13-16

I knew you before I formed you in your mother's womb. Before you were born, I set you apart.

JEREMIAH 1:5

The very hairs on your head are all numbered.

MATTHEW 10:30

REFLECTION

Throughout our lives, there are words spoken to us that
wound us. Maybe they are critical words from a parent or
a spouse. Maybe you've been wounded by a harsh rebuke
from a sibling or a friend. Sometimes we can even harm
each other unintentionally with our words. These wounds
are often as damaging as physical injuries. No matter your
age, you are likely carrying around the unnecessary weight of
someone speaking hurtful words into your life. Today, think
about what words have been said to you and who said them.
Write down the ones that are most painful to you. Will
you give them to Jesus right now? Have you reacted angrily
toward others? Do you need to ask Christ for His forgiveness? Do you need to seek forgiveness from people whom
you've hurt? If there are any hurtful words that keep replaying in your mind, ask Jesus to replace them with His healing
words.

DAILY PRAYER

*Lord Jesus, please help me let go of the words that have hurt
me throughout my life. Please make me aware of how those
hurtful words have kept me from trusting You. In the quiet
moments of my day, I ask You to speak Your truth into my
heart. Heal my wounded heart with Your grace and love this
day. Amen.*

TODAY'S BLESSING

May you allow Jesus to bandage your wounds caused by careless and hurtful words. May you embrace the only voice that matters today. May you hear and accept the love and grace of the heavenly Father who dearly cherishes you and has set you apart as holy. May you trust the words of the One who knew you before you were born.

FOURTEEN

I AM HEALING YOUR INNER VOICES

As you sit here with Me, take note of the tone of the voices and the noise crowding your mind. My child, the truth is your inner life consists of a running conversation that lasts all your waking hours. And that conversation is very important. You actually talk to yourself more than you talk with anyone else in the world. Listen closely to those conversations because they make up your inner life and they also direct your heart. The dialogue you focus on the most will become your reality. You never truly take any action or say any word that isn't born from your inner life.

Your behavior is a direct result of those thoughts you have about yourself and others. Without healing, negative feelings and judgmental words will cause you to hurt others and will isolate you from Me. Quiet yourself for just a moment, and take inventory of your internal words. Reflect on the nature of those words today. Are they filled with the native language of My love for you, brimming with My grace and compassion? Are those inner words coming from My Love Story that was written down for you? Or do those voices speak a language of self-loathing and judgment meant to separate us?

Paul, My apostle, stated that in order for his life to change, he had to *die to his way of thinking* and exchange it for My way of thinking about both himself and the world around him. Remember that you can always change your life with My help. By embracing My love for you, you can cultivate genuine love for yourself that will spill over into the lives of others. You were made to live in My love. You no longer have to be a slave beaten down by the inner words of self-hatred, bitterness, and judgment.

Paul concluded that the renewing of his mind was a process of letting go of his self-centered thoughts and learning how to focus on eternal thoughts based on My words. None of your negative thoughts come from Me; they are not grounded in the truth of My words to you, and so they are not lasting. I encourage you to meditate on the foundations of My Kingdom: love, joy, peace, patience, kindness, goodness, faithfulness, gentleness, and self-control. When you focus your thoughts on these qualities of My Spirit, they will take root in your inner life.

Today, turn your inner dialogue toward these eternal ideas and focus on My nature. My child, you will then begin to experience My unconditional love for you. Study and fill your inner life's conversations with My Word, and they will become your living words of hope. As you meditate on My nature, the grace of My resurrected power will become a part of your life, and you will become fluent in My native language and filled with its abundant joy.

SCRIPTURE

Letting your sinful nature control your mind leads to death. But letting the Spirit control your mind leads to life and peace.

ROMANS 8:6

My old self has been crucified with Christ. It is no longer I who live, but Christ lives in me. So I live in this earthly body by trusting in the Son of God, who loved me and gave himself for me.

GALATIANS 2:20

REFLECTION

As you sit here in prayer and meditation, what conversation is taking place in your inner life? What does that voice sound like? Is it full of self-hatred and judgment? Is it an echo of other people's voices? Or is it full of the fruit of the Spirit: love, joy, peace, patience, kindness, goodness, faithfulness, gentleness, and self-control? Does that conversation reflect the truth of your value in the eyes of the Savior who loves and delights in you? Take some time to document your inner dialogue during the day today. Try to replace any negative words with Scripture you have memorized and with the native language of Christ's love, acceptance, and grace.

DAILY PRAYER

Lord Jesus, please make me aware of the conversation in my inner life this day. Give me discernment to hear Your voice above every other as the guiding light of my life. Heal my self-hatred and judgment, and make me aware of Your eternal love. Allow Your words of life and hope to spring up in my heart and mind and affect my attitude and actions toward others. Amen.

TODAY'S BLESSING

May this day begin a new conversation in your heart and mind that is focused on what is true and eternal. May Christ's voice be heard above all others. May the meditations of your heart produce the fruit that is the foundation of the Kingdom of God. May Jesus direct your words and actions and turn them into blessings for everyone you meet today.

FIFTEEN

I AM HEALING THE PAIN OF YOUR PAST

INVOCATION

Dear Jesus, may I be *still* and *aware* of Your healing
power and forgiving love that are present
with me in this Holy Now.

Dear child, in the moments when you begin to quiet yourself and find Me in the stillness, I know there are a flurry of
thoughts and memories that can hold you prisoner. Those
painful remembrances separate you from the awareness of My
presence with you in this very moment. Maybe they are recol-
lections of hurtful actions that were directed at you. Maybe
they are the things that you have done to hurt others. Maybe
you have remorse for actions that you took or the actions that
you were too afraid to take.

Please realize that regret is only a wasted energy. When you
spend time in those memories, you are being drawn into an
unchangeable past that is far removed from the present reality
of My love. Living in your past will keep you from embracing

the forgiveness I am offering you this very moment. It will hold you back from being present in the beautiful realities of your life today. My child, I came to free you from the despair of constantly reliving your past.

I can heal you from those painful thoughts so that you don't remain forever trapped in the self-imposed prison of your mind. Today, I want you to bring Me the memories that cause you to burn with anger toward those who abused you. I want you to lay down the lingering guilt you have about the times you may have hurt loved ones. I know all the ways you live in remorse and regret, and it is time to surrender them all to Me. I want you to take a breath and meet Me here in this Holy Now.

Those thoughts and images replaying in your mind reveal the unhealed areas in your life, but it is time to stop residing there. It is time for you to release those images. I no longer remember your past, so why do you spend your time there? The more you focus on the past, the more difficult it becomes to enjoy the blessings of life I have for you right now. I no longer want you to be consumed with guilt. I shouldered all your guilt when I went to the cross for you. It is time for you to stop believing that your mistakes are unpardonable— nothing is beyond My forgiveness. Do not diminish the eternal supremacy of My resurrection work by believing the lie that your past is beyond My redemptive power. Instead of dwelling on your failures and sins, turn your full attention to My grace and forgiveness for you.

I can give you power over the past if you will simply embrace My love. In the here and now, you can forgive others and ask for forgiveness. My presence will be powerful when you freely choose to distribute and receive grace. Even if you have to go the extra mile, I want you to work to reconcile and move forward with your life. Learn to forgive yourself and release those who hurt you, just as I have forgiven you. Hold on to Me in this present moment and embrace a life of restoration and right relationships. Relinquish your past to Me and let My love and peace transform your heart.

SCRIPTURE

If you are presenting a sacrifice at the altar in the Temple and you suddenly remember that someone has something against you, leave your sacrifice there at the altar. Go and be reconciled to that person. Then come and offer your sacrifice to God.

MATTHEW 5:23-24

[Christ] personally carried our sins in his body on the cross so that we can be dead to sin and live for what is right. By his wounds you are healed.

I PETER 2:24

REFLECTION

What things from your past do you regret? Are you plagued with guilt about situations that keep replaying in your mind? Do you hang on to grudges against people who have hurt or injured you? Regret and injury are in the past. Jesus is with you right here, in the present moment. He has already forgiven you and already healed you. Are you ready to accept those gifts from Him? Are you ready to release shame and regret and meet Jesus in the Holy Now?

DAILY PRAYER

Lord Jesus, certain words I've said and things I have done in the past are keeping me chained to regret. Please help me to forgive those who have harmed me and to forgive myself for harming others. This day, give me the courage to live a life that reflects Your forgiveness and healing. I am thankful for Your presence and the blessing of Your death and resurrection so I may have eternal life. Amen.

TODAY'S BLESSING

May you go forward with the knowledge that the unchangeable past has been bought and paid for by Jesus on the cross of Calvary. May that truth free you to love and extend the same grace toward others that has been extended to you.

SIXTEEN

I AM HEALING YOUR BODY AND SPIRIT

INVOCATION

Dear Jesus, may I be *still* and *aware* of Your healing
power and forgiving love that are present
with me in this Holy Now.

My child, we must talk candidly about a reality of living in
a fallen world. You may already know that there will be days
of illness and brokenness throughout your life. There will be
times when you are terrified of a diagnosis that your doctors
bring to you. Maybe you were there today in that hospital
room or at a doctor's office receiving unwanted news. It is in
these unsettling moments that I want you to seek Me first.
Please don't allow the fear of the unknown to overwhelm you
in these times of distress. My child, you can trust Me with
your health. I will guide you in the right direction. I can do
My work through prayer and meditation. I can heal you from
the inside out. I want you to believe this day that there are no

limits to My healing power. And I can work with and through doctors, nurses, medical staff, and even their medicines.

Have confidence that I can accomplish miracles and wonders of healing. You can read about it in My Love Story written for you. I cured a blind beggar with some spit and mud. I commanded a paralyzed man to stand up and walk, and instantly he was on his feet. I healed lepers with My words, and their skin became clean before everyone's eyes. I told the sick to rise from their beds, and they were restored to full health. I called my dear friend Lazarus back from death, and he emerged from the tomb in front of many witnesses. And when a crippled man was lowered in front of Me through a roof by loving friends, I made him well. In these times, I want you to surround yourself with the friends and family who will do the same for you. But whenever you are dealing with health issues and pain on your own, I will be present to comfort and walk with you in ways you can only imagine.

But My greatest desire goes far beyond your health today. My ultimate plan is to heal the part of you that lasts forever. I want to make you perfect and whole so we can be together for eternity.

I know you understand that your physical body began dying the moment you were born. It is your soul, the core of your being, that I long to envelop and bring closer to My enduring and consuming love. Yes, My desire for you is so much greater than your physical health—it is to forgive your sins and restore your soul to its intended wholeness and beauty. Your soul—the true reality of who you are—is only beginning to live this very day. When you abide in My love, you are truly freed from all the bonds of sickness and death because I have conquered death. You can toss aside even the most hopeless diagnosis once you embrace the everlasting prognosis of My boundless grace for you.

I want you to take a firm hold on My assurance that no matter what happens, everything will be okay. This day, whatever health setback you are facing, trust Me to always be your Great Physician. Through My love, you have overcome death and will dwell with Me forever.

SCRIPTURE

"I will give you back your health, and heal your wounds," declares the LORD.

JEREMIAH 30:17

He will wipe every tear from their eyes, and there will be no more death or sorrow or crying or pain. All these things are gone forever.

REVELATION 21:4

REFLECTION

We will all face times when sickness weakens our bodies and spirits. We follow a Savior who has overcome death, but He is also the Great Physician. It is difficult at moments to trust Jesus with our everyday illnesses. And yet He cares about each and every one of our needs. Are you willing to let go of the anxiety about your sickness and hand every care over to Jesus? Can you trust Him with your healing? What do you need to surrender to Him today concerning your health? Can you trust Him that no matter what happens, He will walk closely with you every step of the way?

DAILY PRAYER

Lord Jesus, please give me the strength to face my health issues and trust that You are with me. I believe You are the Great Physician who can heal any illness, but no matter what the outcome of my diagnosis is, You are there with me. This day, I pray for healing. Not just physical healing but deep spiritual healing. Restore my body and my soul. Remind me that You have conquered death, and help me take comfort in that truth. Amen.

TODAY'S BLESSING

May you remember that the One who walks and talks with you this day also made the lame walk, commanded the blind to see, and holds power over any illness. May you go forth in the confidence that Jesus has overcome death and is beside you through whatever physical challenge you face this day.

SEVENTEEN

I AM CALMING THE STORMS OF YOUR LIFE

INVOCATION
Dear Jesus, may I be *still* and *aware* of Your healing
power and forgiving love that are present
with me in this Holy Now.

My child, I am forever ready to help and be present with
you during times of trouble. The question I have for you
is simple: Will you allow Me? I have told you that anyone
who tries to save their life will lose it, and anyone who loses
their life in Me will certainly find it. I know how desperately you want to manage the waves of chaos rolling into
your life. But just as My disciples panicked and were terrified during a sudden furious storm, you are cowering in fear
through the tempests of life, wondering how to fix them on
your own.

I know you always want to try to solve your own problems
and find peace. But there is no peace and no true healing

apart from Me. Only I can calm the chaos with a word. When you hesitate to trust and allow Me to help change the course of your life, I will wait patiently for you to exhaust all your other options.

Consider how someone struggling to swim thrashes and flounders and, in the process, makes himself completely unsavable. A drowning person cannot be rescued until he is exhausted from trying to save himself and willing to accept help. Experienced lifeguards know to keep their distance from a flailing swimmer until he or she stops struggling. The key to survival is simply to stop fighting and surrender to the one who is attempting to rescue you.

This lesson is for you this very day as you are tossed back and forth in tumultuous waters. You must let go so that I can come closer. Let Me be your Lifeguard and save you.

I will rescue you from all life's storms when you simply admit there are circumstances you cannot fix on your own. Often, there are times when you will not understand what is happening in your world. It will feel as if you are desperately trying to keep your head above water. In those moments, you must give up control and trust that the solutions are far beyond your power.

When you surrender to Me, you will find My peace. The storm may rage all around you, but you will rest in the still-ness of My presence as you have never rested before. So when you feel you can't handle life any longer, submit everything to Me. Stop fighting against the waves, and believe that I will calm the chaos and still the waters of your life.

SCRIPTURE

Jesus got into the boat and started across the lake with his disciples. Suddenly, a fierce storm struck the lake, with waves breaking into the boat. But Jesus was sleeping. The disciples went and woke him up, shouting, "Lord, save us! We're going to drown!" Jesus responded, "Why are you afraid? You have so little faith!" Then he got up and rebuked the wind and waves, and suddenly there was a great calm.

MATTHEW 8:23-26

If you try to hang on to your life, you will lose it. But if you give up your life for my sake, you will save it.

MATTHEW 16:25

REFLECTION

It is so difficult to admit that you cannot fix your own life. We struggle through the storms of life, trying to stay afloat, when the Creator of the universe is there simply waiting for us to let go and let Him take control. In the midst of turbulent waters, it is counterintuitive to quit fighting and let go, but that is exactly what Jesus wants you to do! Have you tried fixing your problems on your own? How has that worked out? What are you struggling with today that you need to surrender to Christ? What chaotic waters or unidentified fears do you need Jesus to calm? How can you better trust Him to still those storms?

DAILY PRAYER

Lord Jesus, please help me to quit struggling and fighting to save myself. Give me courage to surrender to Your loving guidance and healing peace. Help me to lose my life in You. Amen.

TODAY'S BLESSING

May you stop straining against the chaos in your life and allow God to rescue you. May you release control and lean into the loving arms of Jesus, who can calm the waters of your life. May you simply surrender to Jesus and accept His healing and peace today.

EIGHTEEN

I AM REDEEMING YOUR MISTAKES

INVOCATION
Dear Jesus, may I be *still* and *aware* of Your healing
power and forgiving love that are present
with me in this Holy Now.

My child, everyone makes mistakes. If you have been feeling sorry for yourself today or spent time beating yourself
up because you've messed up, I want to assure you nothing
you can ever do will separate you from My love. In fact, all
your faults and missteps put you in good company. If you
don't think so, let Me remind you about a few of My favorite
people.

Abraham, who was called the father of nations, lied about
his wife twice instead of trusting My Father. Moses, whom
My Father used to deliver the Israelites from slavery, murdered
an Egyptian, but he didn't just stop there. He also ran away
and begged God to find someone "more qualified" to speak
with Pharaoh after being commanded to do the job. Jonah

refused to deliver My Father's message to a city because of his own selfishness, and he needed three nights inside a fish to be convinced otherwise. Elijah, the man who saw My Father bring fire down from the sky, actually hid in a cave when things were tough. And then there is Peter, one of My closest friends, who failed after boasting to everyone that he would never deny knowing Me.

Just read the list of people included in My own family tree, compiled by Matthew, and you will find liars, adulterers, murderers, and even a prostitute—people who made big mistakes at some point in their lives. So whenever you're tempted to feel as if you are too broken or just too messed up to fit into My plans for you, open the pages of My Word, and really pay attention to the lives of the people who did the biggest miracles and accomplished incredible feats in My name.

Now, let's focus on you and your mistakes today. Instead of repeating over and over what you did wrong, just turn it over to Me and forgive yourself. I have told you I am not interested in your past. I only want you to be ready to follow Me right now. To listen to My voice and accept My love. I have forgiven you, and I am restoring and renewing everything in creation—especially you. I only need your willingness to take My hand and move forward into a life of freedom.

If you will surrender your mistakes to Me, I will take and use them to make you better. Your failures will help Me build My Kingdom and redeem the world. Remember that Peter, My disciple who denied Me three times, was exactly who I chose to be the foundation on which I built My church. So don't let your failures and slipups overwhelm you. Don't let your mistakes define you and separate you from Me. I only want you to find your identity in Me, the One who loves you completely, mistakes and all.

SCRIPTURE

He has removed our sins as far from us as the east is from the west.

PSALM 103:12

"But why can't I come now, Lord?" [Peter] asked. "I'm ready to die for you." Jesus answered, "Die for me? I tell you the truth, Peter—before the rooster crows tomorrow morning, you will deny three times that you even know me."

JOHN 13:37-38

I will forgive their wickedness, and I will never again remember their sins.

HEBREWS 8:12

REFLECTION

Everyone makes mistakes. The difference is that the people of God embrace forgiveness and move on from those mistakes. Consider how you have allowed your mistakes to define your life. Think about the fact that God says He doesn't even remember your sins. What do you have in common with the Bible characters who messed up? Have you fallen down or missed the mark in an area of your life? Surrender your mistakes to God and forgive yourself. Then you can get back up and move forward, trusting Jesus to lead you.

DAILY PRAYER

Lord Jesus, take my sins, my mistakes, and my failures, and use them for Your purpose. I am grateful for Your forgiveness today. Please help me to respond to Your grace by getting up and moving forward, following Your calling and purpose for my life. Amen.

TODAY'S BLESSING

May you be emboldened by the truth that the heroes of the Bible were people who made huge mistakes. May you live your life today fully present in each moment, pursuing God's calling for you, redeemed by the forgiveness and grace of the resurrected Jesus.

NINETEEN

SURRENDER YOUR WOUNDED HEART TO ME

INVOCATION
Dear Jesus, may I be *still* and *aware* of Your healing
power and forgiving love that are present
with me in this Holy Now.

I want you to know I see how you have continually searched
the world for solutions, gimmicks, or distractions, hoping you
can find a way to heal your brokenness and pain. I have so
much compassion for you. I understand that you have spent
time and energy looking to others for something you can
only receive from Me. I am asking you to stop, be still, and
acknowledge that the only real and lasting solution is to allow
Me to heal your wounded heart. Whenever you are finally
ready to give up your futile search for other answers, I will be
here, waiting patiently to heal you.

In the meantime, I know your anger and resentfulness are
signs of the scars people have given you. I do not want you
to define your life by your wounds. I want you to find your

identity in Me and accept My love for you. When you are ready, I want you to surrender your wounded heart to Me.

I know how you have suffered, even at the hands of those you trusted. So often, it is those we love who seem to hurt us the most—even when they don't mean to do it. I have witnessed all the ways your wounds have affected how you think about yourself and the way you interact with others. I see how they have eroded your trust. I understand how they have fractured even your closest relationships. I am aware of every time you struggle under the weight of that pain. I know every time you feel defeated and unable to move forward. But I am there in those moments when you are discouraged and hopeless. I will be there when all your efforts to heal or self-medicate fail you. I know your pain because I intimately know and love you.

And I understand the depths of your wounds because I also was misunderstood and rejected by those whom I loved the most. I was crucified by a world I came to save. But I endured everything in order to heal you. You still carry your wounds because you have been looking to others for the unconditional love and healing that only I can give you. My child, the truth is I was wounded so I could fully heal your wounds. Now it is finally time for you to surrender all that pain to Me. You can trust Me with them because I Am your Great Physician. I Am your Good Father. And I Am the only One who loves you perfectly enough to heal your wounded heart. This day, take the steps you need to stop looking for the world to fix you. Quiet yourself in prayer, and surrender it all to Me.

As you embrace My healing, remember those you have injured in your life. As I heal your wounded heart, be thankful and forgive anyone who has hurt you. As I apply the balm of unconditional love, I want you to also forgive and release to Me all those who have damaged you. Bring your wounds to Me, and know I have already endured their torturous sting. Only in Me can you find healing for your wounded heart.

SCRIPTURE

The LORD is close to the brokenhearted; he rescues those whose spirits are crushed.

PSALM 34:18

He heals the brokenhearted and bandages their wounds.

PSALM 147:3

REFLECTION

We live in a broken world and invariably carry wounds from our relationships and life experiences. Jesus wants us to bring our brokenness to Him for healing, but we often look for other ways to treat our wounded hearts. Have you relied on the world's remedies for your broken heart? Have you sought other people for the things that only God can provide? Do you need to forgive someone for the pain that you are carrying around today? Do you need to ask forgiveness for wounding someone? What do you need to do in order to surrender your wounded heart to your Creator? How can you let go of some of those wounds and forgive others?

DAILY PRAYER

Lord Jesus, I ask for Your loving care today. Help me to see others through Your eyes and be compassionate and forgiving. My old wounds have developed thick scars and can only be healed by You. I am grateful for Your healing and want to use its power to forgive everyone who has hurt me. Amen.

TODAY'S BLESSING

May you go into the world with a heart that is restored by the healing power of the resurrected Jesus. May He use your brokenness to heal others. May your wounds be made whole in the power of His holy name this day.

TWENTY

THE HEALING JOY
OF MY PRESENCE

INVOCATION
Dear Jesus, may I be *still* and *aware* of Your healing
power and forgiving love that are present
with me in this Holy Now.

I invite you to find healing joy in My abiding presence. Even
though I've always been by your side, through everything, you
must be fully awake and grounded in this moment to understand that I am truly present with you right now. Yes, you are
on holy ground. As you turn your attention to Me and seek
Me with your whole heart, you will discover My enduring
and all-encompassing love in this Holy Now that will satisfy
the deepest longing in your soul. That satisfaction, My child,
is not some feeling that comes and goes. It is a deep and abiding joy that sustains your entire life. Once you experience the
fullness of My presence, you will never be the same.

I described how to become part of My Kingdom to a
famous religious leader named Nicodemus, who secretly came

to talk with Me under the cover of darkness. Maybe he was like you in some ways, a devout person who thought he knew everything about Me. He believed a relationship with God was following a system of rules and regulations rather than a simple submission—an acknowledgment of My presence and an expression of a profound need for Me. I taught Nicodemus that people are born first of water and then of the Spirit, that life is both physical and spiritual. Now I come to you today and ask you to be born anew in your spirit.

The world in front of you at this very moment appears permanent, but it, too, is passing away. It seems real until you breathe in and open your eyes to the reality that My creative Spirit is the underlying force behind everything that exists. You are made of far more than just flesh and blood. This world around you is grounded in the deeper reality of My eternal Kingdom, with no beginning or end. I Am the One who was there at the beginning, the Word who was with God and was God, and through My power, everything was made and is now being made new again. As you become more aware of this spiritual truth, it will produce joy. And joy, My child, is eternal.

This gift of joy is free for anyone who simply desires to live in the light of My holy presence. I offer you a new way of seeing the world. It is a deep and healing transformation that will allow you to find My fingerprints in all creation. Just embrace My love, and it will transcend and transform every detail of your life. As you become more aware of My presence, you will be moved to follow Me. You will find the boldness to talk and to act like Me, sharing in My work. Surrender your heart to Me today and live in the joy that My presence brings forever.

SCRIPTURE

In the beginning the Word already existed. The Word
was with God, and the Word was God. He existed in the
beginning with God. God created everything through him,
and nothing was created except through him. The Word gave
life to everything that was created, and his life brought light
to everyone.

JOHN 1:1-4

"I tell you the truth, unless you are born again, you cannot
see the Kingdom of God." "What do you mean?" exclaimed
Nicodemus. "How can an old man go back into his mother's
womb and be born again?" Jesus replied, "I assure you, no one
can enter the Kingdom of God without being born of water
and the Spirit. Humans can reproduce only human life, but
the Holy Spirit gives birth to spiritual life. So don't be surprised
when I say, 'You must be born again.'"

JOHN 3:3-7

I have told you these things so that you will be filled with my
joy. Yes, your joy will overflow!

JOHN 15:11

REFLECTION

We spend so much of our lives finding ways to ignore the
presence of Christ, even though that is the one thing we are
longing for the most. It is only through His presence that

we experience a deep and abiding joy. You may have heard the phrase "born again," but have you considered that Jesus wants to bring you joy in His presence? What is the difference between joy and happiness to you? How often do you admit your need for Christ? In what ways are you similar to Nicodemus? How can being present in the moment with Jesus help fill your heart with joy? How can you practice bringing your awareness to the presence of Christ?

DAILY PRAYER

Lord Jesus, I acknowledge Your presence with me in this very moment. I ask for Your healing joy. Help me be renewed and aware of Your enduring love and grace that You give me with each and every breath I take. Amen.

TODAY'S BLESSING

May you discover Christ in the very fabric of all creation. May the joy of being part of His Kingdom mend your heart and soul and permeate every area of your life. May you go and share His healing joy with everyone you meet.

I Am the Way

The Centering Prayer

Dear Jesus, may I be *still* and *aware* of Your teaching
as I sit with You in this Holy Now.

Dear Jesus, may I be *still* and *aware* of Your teaching
as I sit with You.

Dear Jesus, may I be *still* and *aware* of Your teaching.

Dear Jesus, may I be *still* and *aware*.

Dear Jesus, may I be *still*.

Dear Jesus, may I *be*.

TWENTY-ONE

BE SLOW TO JUDGE

INVOCATION

Dear Jesus, may I be still *and* aware *of Your teaching as I sit with You in this Holy Now.*

My child, when I commanded you, "Do not judge," I was speaking about the way you criticize others in your life. You see, it is impossible for you to judge anyone with a pure heart because I Am the only One who knows their true story and the unseen realities of their inner life. When you find yourself focusing on someone else's faults, I want you to be fully aware of your own mistakes and shortcomings and your own need for forgiveness. Did you know that the way you judge others is ultimately how you will be judged?

And I have told you that I don't want you to be guilty of pointing out the speck in your brother or sister's eye all the while ignoring the six-foot log protruding from yours! Yes, it would be wise for you to focus your attention on finding and resolving the issues you carry in your own heart. You know I love you with all your imperfections. So why do you expect others to be perfect before you will offer them love and acceptance?

My grace extends to you, so you need to extend that same grace to others. You cannot know the kind of burdens they may carry today. The angry man you see yelling on the corner may be suffering from an illness. The difficult coworker may be going through a divorce. Even those closest to you are weighed down with problems that you know nothing about. Please remember this whenever you are tempted to criticize them.

Don't join the chorus of hypocrites who expect everyone else in the world to be faultless while they trip and fall with every step. My child, the ugly truth is that if you are constantly judging others, that habit of criticism and condemnation will become embedded in your spirit and you will judge yourself with the same lack of grace. Those who carry around the judge's gavel tend to use it most harshly on themselves. It will darken your heart and leave no room for My unconditional love. Lay down your criticism and learn to see the beauty in the imperfect people all around you. Just as I have made the broken places in your life beautiful, I am also working to do that in the lives of others! Allow Me to replace your thoughts of judgment with contemplations of grace and love.

So let go of the temptation to play the role of judge and jury for other people. Let Me help you see your neighbors through My compassionate eyes. I Am the only One fit to judge the world. And My work on the cross is a grace so scandalous that judgment as you understand it was forever wiped away. Your priority this day is to be most concerned with the work of turning your heart to Me, and then to offer My grace to everyone you meet.

SCRIPTURE

Do not judge others, and you will not be judged. For you will be treated as you treat others. The standard you use in judging is the standard by which you will be judged.

And why worry about a speck in your friend's eye when you have a log in your own? How can you think of saying to your friend, "Let me help you get rid of that speck in your eye," when you can't see past the log in your own eye? Hypocrite! First get rid of the log in your own eye; then you will see well enough to deal with the speck in your friend's eye.

MATTHEW 7:1-5

Do not judge others, and you will not be judged. Do not condemn others, or it will all come back against you. Forgive others, and you will be forgiven.

LUKE 6:37

REFLECTION

When we constantly sit in judgment of those around us, we become distracted from our inner work and Christ's true calling for us to love others. The reality is we only see a small piece of the big picture, even in the people who are closest to us. If we are honest, we know we're not fit to judge anyone.

When we allow our minds to be consumed with evaluating others, it keeps us from accepting the grace Christ offers to us! How have you been judgmental toward others? How does this affect the way you see yourself? How can you make a practice of remembering the unseen burdens that other people carry? What are some practical ways to stop your tendency to self-judge and harbor negative attitudes toward others?

DAILY PRAYER

Lord Jesus, please forgive me for my judgmental attitude toward others. Free me of that habit and release me from self-criticism. Help me to see the beauty of my brokenness and the depth of Your grace for me today. I want to view my neighbors through Your eyes and proclaim how Your scandalous love has changed my life. Amen.

TODAY'S BLESSING

May you offer the world the same love and acceptance that Christ offers you each new morning and with every breath you take. May you lay your judgments at the foot of the cross this day and resolve to gift others with generous grace instead of criticism.

TWENTY-TWO

BE WARY OF YOUR SPIRITUAL PRIDE

INVOCATION
Dear Jesus, may I be *still* and *aware* of Your teaching
as I sit with You in this Holy Now.

Religion can be precarious when you use it as a way to place yourself above those who do not look, act, or talk like you do. You can easily fool yourself into believing you are the only one who possesses the truth. You can be tempted to think you have somehow earned My love! This isn't true faith but a false spirituality based on ego. And the most dangerous part of spiritual pride is that it can subtly sneak into your life. So beware when you feel important because of the way you pray or talk or worship. This pride creates a false sense of superiority, which separates you from others and diverts you from My will for your life. Please be careful whenever you start to think your beliefs or actions put you on My Kingdom guest list.

When you convince yourself that you are part of an exclusive religious in-crowd, you had better remember that My Kingdom isn't built for the in-crowd.

Dear one, I know well that learning to navigate pride is a natural part of being human. Even My closest friends argued about who was the greatest and tried to find ways to distinguish themselves from each other. John and James even dared to ask Me if they could sit at My right and left when I entered My Kingdom. They did not understand the sacrifice that type of honor would require of them. These were My disciples, who had lived with Me for three years, but even they were easily blinded by pride and lost sight of the true nature of My Kingdom.

One day, as a child sat with Me, I shared that anyone who approaches Me with the humility and openheartedness of a child will be great in the Kingdom of God. I wanted to show that if you are not open to showing love to people no matter who they are or where they come from, then you do not truly know Me. My Kingdom isn't about your status! It is the least person among you who is actually the greatest. Yes, the first shall be last. If you truly desire the deep joy of Kingdom living, seek to be a servant!

When you take up your cross and follow Me, you must give up everything in the name of sacrificial love. My Kingdom is an upside-down Kingdom where you must become powerless to be entrusted with eternal power. The cross is a symbol of a holy brokenness that allowed My light to burst through the Temple veil that separated us. You did nothing to earn it!

So be wary whenever you are tempted to feel prideful about your spiritual life. Following Me requires deep humility and persistent sacrifice. When you identify with the least of these, who can never offer you anything in return, you will identify with Me. Come to Me in each new moment with the humility and open heart of a child. Yes, humble yourself and embrace service to others, and you will be among the greatest in My Kingdom.

SCRIPTURE

For even the Son of Man came not to be served but to serve others and to give his life as a ransom for many.
MARK 10:45

[Jesus'] disciples began arguing about which of them was the greatest. But Jesus knew their thoughts, so he brought a little child to his side. Then he said to them, "Anyone who welcomes a little child like this on my behalf welcomes me, and anyone who welcomes me also welcomes my Father who sent me. Whoever is the least among you is the greatest."
LUKE 9:46-48

A man sitting at the table with Jesus exclaimed, "What a blessing it will be to attend a banquet in the Kingdom of God!" Jesus replied with this story: "A man prepared a great feast and sent out many invitations. . . . But [the guests] all began making excuses. . . . The servant returned and told his master what they had said. His master was furious and said, 'Go quickly into the streets and alleys of the town and invite the poor, the crippled, the blind, and the lame.' After the servant had done this, he reported, 'There is still room for more.' So his master said, 'Go out into the country lanes and behind the hedges and urge anyone you find to come, so that the house will be full. For none of those I first invited will get even the smallest taste of my banquet.'"

LUKE 14:15-16, 18, 21-24

REFLECTION

It is so easy to get caught up in spiritual pride without even thinking about it. So many of the ways we worship can actually keep us from experiencing the presence of Jesus. We can often become prideful about how we pray, act, talk, or worship, and we can easily forget that we did nothing to earn the gift of salvation! Think about the ways that you have become full of yourself in your religious life. What do you need to surrender to Christ in order to be humble and openhearted like a child? How can you practice more humility, curiosity, and love in your daily life? What are you actively doing for the "least of these" in your neighborhood? Who can you be a servant for today?

DAILY PRAYER

Lord Jesus, please forgive me for the times that my pride has come between us. Teach me to approach You like a child, with wonder, innocence, and humility. Show me the areas of my life where I have allowed spiritual pride to separate me from Your will for me. Amen.

TODAY'S BLESSING

May you live with childlike curiosity, humility, and love toward God and the people in your life. May you let go of the pride that has invaded your spiritual practices and be renewed today by the Spirit of God. In these moments, may you experience the God of the universe with new eyes.

TWENTY-THREE

DON'T WORRY ABOUT TOMORROW

INVOCATION
Dear Jesus, may I be *still* and *aware* of Your teaching
as I sit with You in this Holy Now.

Don't waste any more time or energy worrying about the
future, My child. Worry only robs you of the joy and excitement of the moment. When you are consumed with anxieties
about what tomorrow may bring, you have little room for
faith. Rest in the truth that My love for you is beyond what
you can even imagine, and don't lose sleep over what may
happen to you and your loved ones. I know one of the greatest fears and uncertainties you can face during your time on
earth is about your own death. It will take focused time in
prayer to surrender that fear to Me.

I want you to live confidently each day with the assurance that you can overcome *whatever* the world throws at
you. I know these times are full of troubling news that cause

you apprehension and distress. But much of your fretting is about things that will never actually come to pass. You will always find a reason to fear when you project yourself out of this moment and into the unknown. Living consumed with fears about the future will only flood your mind with trepidation, turning your attention away from My presence. Bring Me your fear, and I can transform it into an eternal hope for living.

You can spend so much time avoiding or suppressing those deep-seated fears and worries about tomorrow. The reality is that your life on earth is temporary, and yet death no longer has the final say—it is simply a gateway into the permanence of My presence. There is no need to be anxious once you understand that death is not the end but a beautiful transition into a new realm of living. Remember, you are My child, and I have liberated you from the absurdity and finality of death.

I have commanded you not to worry about what you will eat or drink or wear tomorrow. You cannot add a second to your life by worrying. So do not allow the fear of anything to cause you to miss out on living life to the fullest right now. The treasure within you is the gift of My resurrection power that gives you everlasting life and eternal hope through My Spirit. Distress and worry will steal even momentary peace. Trust Me with your doubts, and I will hold your reservations about the future in My capable hands.

I Am the Alpha and the Omega—the Beginning of everything and the End of everything. Your future, just like this present moment, belongs to Me. Do not be afraid, for I am with you now and forever beyond time. Understand, My child, that fear and worry can only dislodge you from the reality of the sacred moment that is right before you. Be present and receive the gift of grace, joy, and love I offer you in this Holy Now.

SCRIPTURE

That is why I tell you not to worry about everyday life— whether you have enough food and drink, or enough clothes to wear. Isn't life more than food, and your body more than clothing? Look at the birds. They don't plant or harvest or store food in barns, for your heavenly Father feeds them. And aren't you far more valuable to him than they are? Can all your worries add a single moment to your life?

MATTHEW 6:25-27

Don't worry about tomorrow, for tomorrow will bring its own worries. Today's trouble is enough for today.

MATTHEW 6:34

O death, where is your victory? O death, where is your sting? For sin is the sting that results in death, and the law gives sin its power. But thank God! He gives us victory over sin and death through our Lord Jesus Christ.

I CORINTHIANS 15:55-57

REFLECTION

How many moments of your day are lost because you are consumed with fears and worries about some future event you cannot control? Maybe you are afraid something might happen to you or a loved one. Today, whenever you are tempted to project into the future, gently bring your attention back to the moment and ask God to help you focus on what is in front of you. How can you learn to trust God with the future? Make a list of the fears and concerns that sidetrack you from the life God has for you and offer that list to Him in prayer. Practice reciting a Scripture or prayer that can help you dwell on Christ whenever worries overwhelm you.

DAILY PRAYER

Lord Jesus, remind me this day that You are the Author of my life. Show me how much You love me. I give You my present and my future. Forgive me for missing out on the beauty all around me when I obsess on what might happen weeks or months from now. Help me surrender my fears to You and be fully aware of Your presence with me in each moment of my day. Amen.

TODAY'S BLESSING

May you live today full of boldness and complete confidence that God is always with you—now and in the uncertain future. May the assurance of God's everlasting love be a beacon that shines through you to the world. May you be present in the Holy Now and deeply aware of how Christ provides you with everything you need—just the right amount at just the right time.

TWENTY-FOUR

LET GO OF YOUR BUSYNESS AND HURRY

INVOCATION

Dear Jesus, may I be *still* and *aware* of Your teaching
as I sit with You in this Holy Now.

It is so easy to get swept away in the frantic, busy pace of your
life and lose awareness of My presence. You are rushing around
so fast that you cannot hear My voice. My child, I know you
have schedules to keep and deadlines to meet. But when you
choose to measure your life with clocks and checklists, you pay
a price with stress, fatigue, and even illness. You will find yourself on the edge of insanity with frayed nerves and a flaring
temper. And what is your hurry? Where will all the busyness
really get you? Do you really believe I love you for what you
do? You spend the majority of your time focusing on things
that are far from eternal. Whether you realize it or not, the
time you spend with Me is your most precious possession.

I want you to pause, take a deep breath, clear your schedule, and unplug from your gadgets and devices. Set aside the

long list of activities you think you should be getting done. Don't allow others to impose their expectations on you, which only steal your time and your energy. Let's be honest, much of your busyness and hurry is actually pointless. I did not intend for you to live life at full speed. And I don't want you to lose touch with Me and what I want to do in your heart.

Feeling busy all the time will make you lose connection with Me and the lasting peace that only My presence can provide you. When you are in a hurry, you miss so much of the beauty I have placed in your life. Remember how My friend Martha rushed from one task to another? Her busyness was actually a distraction keeping her from the eternal gift of simply being in My presence. My child, I don't love you for what you do. There is a time for doing. But in order to know Me, you must also learn to be still. Just be still and let Me love you.

So I command you to slowly breathe into this sacred moment. Take a quiet walk and talk with Me. You will experience My comfort, and I will provide you the rest and perspective you need to get through each day. Lay your list of tasks at My feet and let Me direct your actions. Make your time with Me your first priority. Focus on My presence in the stillness of this Holy Now, and I will bring peace and restoration to your chaotic life. I am the unshakable and unchanging God who is absolutely reliable and trustworthy. Let My presence calm your mind and hold your life in place.

SCRIPTURE

Have you never heard? Have you never understood? The LORD is the everlasting God, the Creator of all the earth. He never grows weak or weary. No one can measure the depths of his understanding. He gives power to the weak and strength to the powerless. Even youths will become weak and tired, and young men will fall in exhaustion. But those who trust in the LORD will find new strength. They will soar high on wings like eagles. They will run and not grow weary. They will walk and not faint.

ISAIAH 40:28-31

Jesus said, "Come to me, all of you who are weary and carry heavy burdens, and I will give you rest. Take my yoke upon you. Let me teach you, because I am humble and gentle at heart, and you will find rest for your souls.

MATTHEW 11:28-29

Jesus said, "Let's go off by ourselves to a quiet place and rest awhile." He said this because there were so many people coming and going that Jesus and his apostles didn't even have time to eat.

MARK 6:31

REFLECTION

In today's world, busyness and hurry are almost a badge of honor. But when we are running here and there, caught up in the hectic pace of life, there is often little room for Christ. The Bible commands us to "be still, and know" (Psalm 46:10). Have you busied yourself with unnecessary activities that you should say no to? Have you fallen into the trap of measuring yourself by how busy you are or what you accomplish? What are you in a hurry to do today that doesn't need to be done? What checklist can you throw away? What else do you need to do in order to slow down, breathe, and simply be present with Jesus right now?

DAILY PRAYER

Lord Jesus, please show me the areas in my life where I need to slow down, be still, and be present with You. I want the deep peace that only comes with the awareness of Your presence. Provide me with the wisdom and courage to step out of the busyness and hurry of life and focus my attention fully on You. Amen.

TODAY'S BLESSING

May you be deeply aware of the presence of God today in the calm and quiet spaces of your life. May you boldly say no to the things of life that do not matter and say yes to the moments that are eternal. May you be present with Christ and find the peace that only He can provide.

TWENTY-FIVE

WEALTH AND POPULARITY ARE EMPTY DREAMS

INVOCATION

Dear Jesus, may I be *still* and *aware* of Your teaching
as I sit with You in this Holy Now.

I know that, everywhere you turn, you are faced with the temptation to get noticed or the persistent lure of getting rich. Do not listen to the voices or believe the pictures that tell you happiness is a result of accumulating money or being popular. Building wealth and gathering followers will only bring more complexity into your life. I know it can be challenging to make it through an hour without being enticed to believe that you are missing out on something that will make you feel whole. But those cravings for security and acceptance cannot be satisfied by this transient world. The pleasure and satisfaction you receive from money and popularity will last for a fleeting moment and then vanish forever. But pursuing My will for you brings eternal joy. The only true everlasting refuge is found in Me.

No matter how frugal or hardworking you are, worldly wealth can never bring you real security. I want you to focus instead on storing up your eternal wealth. Nothing you gather on this earth can go with you into eternity. Your life is like a vapor—you are here one day and gone the next. So the more you give away to others, the more wealth you will build in My Kingdom. So commit to being generous with what you have! Remember how difficult it was for the rich young man to leave his wealth behind and follow Me? And yet the poorest widow with just a few coins willingly gave everything she had. This is much deeper than money; where your priorities are, there your heart is also.

Also, do not look for others to praise you. If too many people in the world think you are great, there is a good chance you are not following Me. If I have blessed you with popularity, then you have a great responsibility to humbly reflect My love and grace for all your followers to witness. Make sure that you apply your influence to help those who are less fortunate. You will be held accountable for how you use the temporal frills of your time on earth. Don't put any of it ahead of your relationship with Me.

In these matters, it is so important to quiet yourself, listen for My voice, and let My commands influence your worldly ambitions. Spend time alone with Me, and I will feed your soul. The more you are filled with My Spirit, the less you will be moved by the desires of your ego. When you use your time on earth to accumulate fortune or impress others, you will always be forced to compromise your soul's truest identity. Your unique value is found only in My love. If you look to wealth or recognition for security and satisfaction, you will quickly learn how empty and alone these pursuits will leave you. Joy cannot be purchased. No amount of adoration from other people will bring you the peace your soul desires. My child, do not expect to receive from the world what only I can give. Instead, trust Me to provide what you need. Open your heart, focus on Me, and enjoy the riches of eternal life today.

SCRIPTURE

For the love of money is the root of all kinds of evil. And some people, craving money, have wandered from the true faith and pierced themselves with many sorrows.

1 TIMOTHY 6:10

What causes fights and quarrels among you? Don't they come from your desires that battle within you? You desire but do not have, so you kill. You covet but you cannot get what you want, so you quarrel and fight. You do not have because you do not ask God.

JAMES 4:1-2, NIV

REFLECTION

Every day, we are tempted to idolize money and popularity. Moment by moment, we are presented with the long list of the things we do not possess, the people we do not know, and the influence we do not have. The Bible tells us that things like wealth and celebrity are not eternal and that we should seek Christ's Kingdom first. Have you placed too much emphasis on financial security in your life? Do you value how well-liked you are by others more than your relationship with Christ? Are you faithful with what God has given you? How can you look to Christ for security and satisfaction instead of looking to the world?

DAILY PRAYER

Lord Jesus, please give me the perspective today to make sure my priorities, my hopes, and my desires are grounded in Your approval only. Remind me that the treasure I seek is You, not anything I accumulate in this world. Thank You for the gift of Your love and the material gifts You have given me. Help me to be generous with everything I have. Amen.

TODAY'S BLESSING

May you live free of the illusion that wealth and popularity can bring you deep and lasting joy. May you handle your earthly blessings in a way that reflects the love and generosity of Christ. May you be filled with the contentment that only comes from His abiding presence and love.

TWENTY-SIX

LET ME GUARD THE WORDS OF YOUR MOUTH

INVOCATION

Dear Jesus, may I be *still* and *aware* of Your teaching as I sit with You in this Holy Now.

I want to challenge you to consider how you talk to others and be mindful of the language you use. Words are so important. My Father spoke the universe into existence with a few words. I commanded the lame to walk and the blind to see, and even raised Lazarus from the dead with My words. I remind you of these things because I want you to be aware that words—even yours—carry great power and should be used thoughtfully.

So be considerate whenever you speak. I understand it is so easy to talk carelessly or become tangled up in gossip. It is human nature to engage in stories that accentuate the troubles and weaknesses of other people. Everyone loves to be the storyteller and the center of attention. But you should always be mindful of My Word to you that what comes out of your mouth actually reveals the condition of your heart. The things that you say reflect what is truly happening in your inner being. Your words are the truest measure of the temperature of your soul.

Talking about others is often a way to avoid being honest about yourself. If you quiet yourself and reflect, you will find that you often get caught up in gossip in order to avoid the conversations I really want to have with you. You see, when you spend time talking about others, it helps you hide and deny the shortcomings and failures you deal with every day in your life. But your words have weight, capable of healing or destroying another person.

You must learn to tame your words. It is a daily practice just like talking with Me or reading Scripture. Simply be careful not to mention something about someone that you wouldn't be comfortable saying to the person face-to-face. Stop yourself when you are tempted to tell your side of the story, even when other people have attacked your character. Remember to let Me be your defense attorney! And don't tolerate gossip about someone who is not present in the conversation. You may hurt the character of another person simply by giving silent assent to the damning words spoken about them. If you cannot provide a good report about someone, move on to another subject altogether. Let your conversations center on eternal things that have lasting value. Cling to My words and do your best not to let others define you or anyone else in a negative way.

Gossip is as dangerous as it is easy. My friend, just as you wouldn't do physical harm to anyone, do your best not to damage people with your words either. I encourage you to control your tongue and invite Me to guard the words you speak. When you take this precaution, you are protecting your own heart. Be slow to speak ill of others, and you will be blessed with deep relationships. Meditate on the fruit of My Spirit—love, joy, peace, patience, kindness, goodness, faithfulness, gentleness, and self-control—and you will find them reflected in your words.

Let My love shape your vocabulary. If you meditate on My peace, love, and joy in your heart, then that is the dialect that will emerge in your conversations. Most of all, before you speak, My child, prayerfully consider whether your words are life-giving or damaging. My words bring new life and create peace. Let your words be clear evidence of My work in your heart as you speak My peace into the world.

SCRIPTURE

Take control of what I say, O LORD, and guard my lips.

PSALM 141:3

The tongue can bring death or life; those who love to talk will reap the consequences.

PROVERBS 18:21

These people honor me with their lips, but their hearts are far from me.

MATTHEW 15:8

REFLECTION

The Bible tells us that words are powerful. After all, God spoke the world into existence. But we are commanded to be careful with our own words. What do your conversations reflect about the condition of your heart today? Are you thoughtful about what you say to others? Have you had verbal conflict with someone for which you need to ask forgiveness? Have you participated in spreading gossip or simply sat quietly when someone else did? What does it mean to surrender your words to Christ today? How can you discipline yourself to speak life into other people? How can you use your words to spread the peace of Christ in the world?

DAILY PRAYER

Lord Jesus, forgive me for the words I have used that may have hurt others. I surrender my heart to You and pray that it would be filled with the fruit of Your Spirit. I want my words to be a reflection of Your work in my life, a blessing that brings hope and light and peace to all who hear them. Amen.

TODAY'S BLESSING

May you speak light into the world with everything you say. May your words have God's signature of love embedded in each syllable. May your heart's vocabulary reflect Christ, who is working through your life to bring peace to the world.

TWENTY-SEVEN

LOVE AND PRAY FOR YOUR ENEMIES

INVOCATION

Dear Jesus, may I be *still* and *aware* of Your teaching as I sit with You in this Holy Now.

I know that My most difficult command for you is to love your enemies and pray for those who want to persecute you or do you harm. My child, that command may seem like an impossible task at times. Remember that I have told you to pick up your cross in order to follow Me. I never promised this path would be easy. So even when loving your neighbor is the last thing you want to do, take heart—you are not facing this alone. No matter how difficult your circumstances, remember that I have already overcome the world. And even this most demanding of my instructions is given out of concern for your heart. You see, when you love your enemies, you are participating in a supernatural act that doesn't just change the very order and foundations of the world—it also changes you.

You have heard Me say you should turn the other cheek when someone strikes you. That can sound nearly impossible at times. But it breaks My heart when this powerful teaching is used by religious people to justify exploitation. My words are not meant to keep you under the authority of abusive people. I want you to listen carefully and always remember that I never want you to stay in places or in relationships where you are being physically or emotionally harmed. My instructions are intended for your freedom and the well-being of your soul, My child.

My love will never threaten or diminish who you are! Understand the truth that you have eternal grace and power when you refuse to return one violent act with another. Walking away from violence, turning the other cheek, transforms those moments and makes them holy. Through everything that was ever done to Me, I was always one word away from commanding legions of angels to come to My side. But I went through the worst physical and emotional violence anyone could experience because of My love not just for you but also for your enemies. I wanted to show the world that lasting change only happens through My sacrificial love. Nothing good ever comes from verbal and physical violence. When you have been struck on one cheek, standing strong and offering your other is an act of holy defiance. You are embracing the fullness of My resurrection power when you do that!

My child, in those difficult situations, you are a divine model of strength showing the entire world that the cycle of violence ends with you. You are acknowledging through the pain that you are more than just flesh and blood; you have overcome the world through Me. And if you face these difficult moments, remember that I am right there by your side. When your enemies strike you, they also strike Me.

When I command you to love your enemies, I am doing so out of concern for your soul. When you pray for your enemies, it may not change who they are, but it does reorient *your* heart, and it changes who you are on the inside. Through My eyes, you will begin to see how broken even the worst of your enemies are. You will discover compassion for them and their misguided way of life.

You are precious to Me, and I care deeply for you. When you trust Me for salvation, you are safe and secure in My hands. The secret to loving your enemies is found in your willingness to surrender to the power of My unconditional love for you . . . and for them. It will not be through your strength that you do this but through Mine.

SCRIPTURE

But I say, do not resist an evil person! If someone slaps you on the right cheek, offer the other cheek also.

MATTHEW 5:39

But I say, love your enemies! Pray for those who persecute you!

MATTHEW 5:44

There is no greater love than to lay down one's life for one's friends.

JOHN 15:13

REFLECTION

The command to love your enemies and to pray for those who persecute you may feel like the most demanding of Christ's instructions. But consider today how doing this can actually change your heart. Remember that this doesn't require you to stay in a situation where you are being harmed or abused. It is actually about embracing the fullness of Christ's resurrection power! So who do you need to be praying for today? In what situation do you need the strength to stand strong and turn the other cheek? How can your commitment to love your enemies change your neighborhood? How can you end the cycle of verbal or physical violence in your world?

DAILY PRAYER

Lord Jesus, be with me in the most difficult moments of discipleship, when I have to love people who potentially could harm me. Give me strength to trust You to protect me. Help me to see my enemies through Your eyes in all their brokenness, and give me the words to pray for them. Come close to me this day and fill me with Your resurrection power and love. Remind me I am safe in Your eternal hands. Amen.

TODAY'S BLESSING

May you boldly go forth knowing that Christ has conquered the cycle of violence in the world. May you pray for those who wish to harm you, and may you allow your heart to be transformed by the sacrificial love of Jesus. May you react with grace when you are wronged, turning the other cheek in the name of Christ.

TWENTY-EIGHT

RUN AWAY FROM A SAFE LIFE

INVOCATION
Dear Jesus, may I be *still* and *aware* of Your teaching
as I sit with You in this Holy Now.

My child, suffering will be a reality in your life, but I do not
want you to run and hide from it or ever try to play it safe! I
know that many of My followers have been misled and struggle
to make sense of their relationship with Me when the world
around them gets tough. Sometimes, they are even tempted to
hide behind church doors! Maybe you've been taught that once
you have come to know Me, you will no longer be negatively
impacted by the broken circumstances of the world in which
you live. I have offered everyone the free will to choose or to
reject Me, and as long as there are people who reject love, there
will be brokenness and suffering that touch everyone. So please
don't fall for the idea that once you enter into relationship with
Me, you will become immune from suffering! Remember how
I have called you to take up your cross and follow Me.

We are doing the work of rebuilding a broken world and renewing a creation that has lost its way. This is not easy work—real love is a costly endeavor. And even though you are surrounded by My presence and love, you will still face sickness, persecution, and many difficulties. When you are truly following Me, the road ahead will not be an easy street. Yes, I Am your Good King, but I never promised that you would live a fortunate and worry-free life. In fact, following Me on the path of sacrificial love is anything but a life of safety! It is a life filled with joy, excitement, grace, and deep contentment even in the midst of chaos and turmoil.

I have promised you eternal life. If you accept this gift from Me, it will begin right now, with your next breath, and it will carry you into My presence here on earth and forever. Suffering is a human reality. If you can learn to walk hand in hand with Me through that suffering, I can show you how those difficult times will only perfect your soul and bring you a joy that cannot be taken away.

Do not barricade your heart or hide away your love for Me. Instead let your love burn bright for all to see. Using religious language, church walls, or political power to shelter yourself from the world will only separate you from My love. My love for you is greatest when it is being shared with others. It is not a love that can be hid away like buried treasure. It must be invested in the lives of those around you. When you build self-imposed cocoons and create safety nets, you are actually abandoning your trust in Me.

My cross is the turning point of the world and the catalyst of your salvation. There is no safe or risk-free existence in this world when you are living in My perfect will. Open your heart to the sick, the poor, and the brokenhearted in your own neighborhood. If you open your eyes, you'll experience spiritual growth when you face calamity or suffer loss. Don't spend your life trying to avoid hardships or become bitter when things don't go your way. Instead, grasp My hand to meet those challenges, and you will be transformed from the inside out. Even in your darkest hours, let your brokenness lead you into the fullness of My presence. You must risk everything to find a life worth living. Follow Me into a life where safety ends and love truly begins.

SCRIPTURE

[Jesus] said to the crowd, "If any of you wants to be my follower, you must give up your own way, take up your cross daily, and follow me."

LUKE 9:23

We can rejoice, too, when we run into problems and trials, for we know that they help us develop endurance.

ROMANS 5:3

Be thankful in all circumstances, for this is God's will for you who belong to Christ Jesus.

I THESSALONIANS 5:18

REFLECTION

Jesus teaches throughout Scripture that we are not to hide our faith away but to invest it in the world around us. He calls us to take up our cross—an instrument of execution—and follow Him. That commitment means we are to die to ourselves. And there is no exemption from suffering when you make that decision. How do those realizations inform the way you are living your life today? Have you allowed Christ to work through your suffering? When we are most present with Christ, He becomes visible to the world around us. Is that the type of faith you are living? Do you expect following Jesus will protect you from the circumstances of a fallen world? Are you holding on to bitterness about your own suffering? How can you let go of playing it safe in your daily life?

DAILY PRAYER

Lord Jesus, I realize I will encounter hardships in life. I know that following Your will can put me in harm's way. I recognize that suffering is a part of living. Give me the courage today to pick up my cross and follow You. Show me the ways You are calling me from safety and into contentment and joy. Amen.

TODAY'S BLESSING

May you live fearlessly today and resist adopting a hollow, safe life. May you experience the full and eternal joy of following Christ. May you face the trials and tribulations of a fallen world with the knowledge that Christ is perfecting you and those around you through these difficulties.

TWENTY-NINE

WALK GENTLY IN THE LIVES OF OTHERS

Dear Jesus, may I be *still* and *aware* of Your teaching
as I sit with You in this Holy Now.

My child, I urge you not to spend your time dwelling on
other people's words and actions. When you center your
attention on someone else's conduct, it will only draw you
away from Me and what I want to do in your life. You have
enough to manage on your own, so do not be bothered with
what other people are doing! And please be careful when
you are tempted to tell other people what to do. Just as I
have never coerced you into doing anything, you must never
manipulate anyone else using My name.

Think about the miraculous way I am working in your
life each moment. Think of the ways that I am changing your
heart and your attitude toward others. Consider how patient

and loving I am with you. You need to trust that I am doing the same in the lives of others.

I know it is natural for you to want to correct people when you think they are doing something wrong. I know it can be so easy to validate your anger toward the people who may have hurt you in some way. But you must remember that I am in control. I Am the Good Teacher. When I commanded you not to take My name in vain, it was a stern warning not to try to manipulate others using My authority. I had strong words for anyone who led people astray in My name. I said that it would be better for such a person to be thrown into the sea with a millstone tied around their neck!

So when you see a brother or sister stumble, remember the times when you have fallen. How did you feel inside? Did you need a lecture? Or would you have appreciated a helping hand to get you back on your feet? I want you to walk with grace and compassion in the lives of others because I offer you the same treatment. Rest in the assurance that I bore all the trials you can ever experience on My way to the cross. Even when you make mistakes, you know I have already forgiven and forgotten them. I command you to do the same with the people in your life. Spend less time sermonizing, more time loving them, and you will be closer to fulfilling My will.

I understand how powerless you may feel when the people you love make the wrong decisions. But I've watched you do the same. I know all about the broken promises and agonizing relationships in your life. I have experienced that brokenness too. If you will look to Me for the love and assurance you need, and if you will learn to trust Me to work in the lives of others, I will free you from the temptation to manipulate them. Only I can free you to love them without expectation, and I will add power to your prayers for them. My journey to the cross was an act of unconditional love that did not weigh your sins or failures. Just as I will never invade your life uninvited, I ask you to do the same with the people in your life. Wait in loving expectation for them as I have done with you. Live a life of freedom and forgiveness, and you will see how it shines My light into their world. Always walk gently in the lives of others and be quick to share with them the endless grace that I have offered you.

SCRIPTURE

You must not misuse the name of the LORD your God. The LORD will not let you go unpunished if you misuse his name.
EXODUS 20:7

Make allowance for each other's faults, and forgive anyone who offends you. Remember, the Lord forgave you, so you must forgive others.
COLOSSIANS 3:13

REFLECTION

It can be so tempting to try to influence other people when they aren't doing what you think they should do. But paying attention to what other people are doing is a distraction from our own lives. The Bible teaches us to be careful when we speak direction into the lives of others—especially when we do it in God's name. Christ calls us to live a life that reflects

His grace and love. Have you considered the grace Christ has extended to you—that while you were still a sinner, He died for you? Have you extended that grace to others? Have you used God's name to sway someone to do what you wanted them to do? In what ways do you need to walk more gently in the lives of other people?

DAILY PRAYER

Lord Jesus, forgive me for the ways that I have lost trust in You and tried to influence the actions of other people, especially when it benefited me. Provide me with unwavering trust in the good work You are accomplishing in other people just as You are doing in my life. Remind me of Your endless grace and prompt me to offer that same grace to those in my life this day. Amen.

TODAY'S BLESSING

May you live free from trying to control others and be gracious to everyone you meet. May you trust Christ's work in other people and not be tempted to use His name to influence them. May your heart be so full of Christ's unconditional love that people take notice. May you walk gently in the lives of others this day.

THIRTY

EVERLASTING PEACE BEGINS WITH YOU

INVOCATION

Dear Jesus, may I be *still* and *aware* of Your teaching
as I sit with You in this Holy Now.

Peace. I understand that it sounds like an impossible idea these days. The world is so filled with chaos, discord, and hatred that the idea of brokenness being restored to wholeness, and disharmony replaced by harmony, seems like a giant fairy tale. I know that you hear governments talking about peace. Intelligent and powerful people hold meetings at world summits to plan for it. And, of course, songs and poems have been written about the dream of peace for centuries. You may be thinking, *What does peace really have to do with me?* You may even feel cynicism when you hear the word. I am here to tell you, My child, that peace in the world is here, and it expands with each and every decision you make to love others.

The power of My Kingdom lies in your awareness of My

loving presence. In the stillness of your heart, peace begins to permeate every area of your life. And once My peace grows deep roots in your own heart, it will reach out like strong vines into the hearts of others. Peace will stretch out into your neighborhood and beyond. My child, that is how peace truly grows—from one heart to the next. The truth is that the Everlasting Peace of My Kingdom, which began with an empty tomb, will someday cover all creation.

When you choose to love Me with all your heart, all your mind, all your strength, and all your soul, I will teach you how to love your neighbor. When you experience intimate communion with Me, you will become more and more aware that you are created in My image just like every other person on earth. You will begin to see how deeply you are connected to all My creation. I came to save the world, the whole world, with My sacrificial love. My victory on the cross was for all creeds, colors, and nations of people—beginning with you.

Hear My command this day that, just as I have loved you, you should love others. And because I first loved you, you can know and understand the depth of My sacrificial love. Peace begins with accepting My grace into your life. It will grow as you practice forgiveness, letting go of the bitterness, anger, and resentment that separate you from My love. Only when you discover inner peace in your own soul can you be at peace with those around you.

So seek My never-ending love, and it will be given to you. Through Me, you can find grace and love for your neighbor and discover the humility to love yourself. This is the day I want you to embrace the truth that peace truly begins with you. Peace is not some unattainable dream. I did not overcome death to call you into a life of cynicism! As you have received My love, you are now a peacemaker, carrying the reality of My Kingdom with you wherever you go. My peaceable Kingdom is yours to share.

SCRIPTURE

When people's lives please the LORD, even their enemies are at peace with them.

PROVERBS 16:7

Blessed are the peacemakers, for they will be called children of God.

MATTHEW 5:9, NIV

We love each other because he loved us first. If someone says, "I love God," but hates a fellow believer, that person is a liar; for if we don't love people we can see, how can we love God, whom we cannot see? And he has given us this command: Those who love God must also love their fellow believers.

1 JOHN 4:19-21

REFLECTION

Peace, especially in today's fractured world, seems unreachable. But Scripture tells us that peace begins in our hearts. Christ called us to be peacemakers and promised that the Kingdom would be ours. *Shalom*, the Hebrew word for "peace," represents the ideas of harmony, wholeness, completeness, prosperity, welfare, and tranquility. Where do you see the need for those aspects of peace in your life or the lives of others? Do you find the peace of Christ when you spend time in prayer and meditation? Are you cynical about the idea of peace in the world? What does peace mean to you in this moment? What area of your heart needs peace today? Who in your life needs the peace of Christ right now? What can you do to bring peace to your neighbors?

DAILY PRAYER

Lord Jesus, please show me the areas in my life that lack Your peace. Make me aware of Your deep and abiding love, and infuse me with Your peace. Help me see the need for peace in my heart and in my neighbors' lives. Forgive me for holding on to cynicism or prejudice. Forgive me for judging others and causing separation between us. May I be an effective peacemaker in Your holy name. Amen.

TODAY'S BLESSING

May you sit in the presence of the resurrected Jesus and accept His peace in your life this day. May you be an ambassador of peace to everyone. May the peace that grows in your heart reach into your neighborhood and change the world. May peace begin with you this moment.

I Am the Promise

The Centering Prayer

Dear Jesus, may I be *still* and *aware* of Your enduring promise to me as I abide with You in this Holy Now.

Dear Jesus, may I be *still* and *aware* of Your enduring promise to me as I abide with You.

Dear Jesus, may I be *still* and *aware* of Your enduring promise.

Dear Jesus, may I be *still* and *aware*.

Dear Jesus, may I be *still*.

Dear Jesus, may I *be*.

THIRTY-ONE

TURNING BROKENNESS INTO DIVINE ART

INVOCATION

Dear Jesus, may I be *still* and *aware* of Your enduring promise to me as I abide with You in this Holy Now.

My child, come to Me with your shattered hopes and broken dreams. I know that life will inevitably bring heartbreaks. I understand that there will be times when your life seems like a stained-glass window shattered into jagged shards, lying in disarray. There will be moments when everything feels broken. Maybe you are in the midst of a crashing marriage. Perhaps your health is fragile. Maybe a longtime friendship has been fractured, or you are on the verge of financial ruin. There will be a time when you wonder if there is any hope for putting your life back together. This is life in a fallen world where people are free to refuse My love. But take heart, My child. I promise you that broken things are My favorite canvas to work with! And you are My most prized project.

In the seasons of brokenness, you will feel anger. You will

have so many questions that seem unanswerable. There may be times when you believe that even death would be easier for you to handle! The open wounds of rejection and the sense of abandonment and failure that brokenness can bring into your life can be a heavy burden to carry by yourself. I want you to be honest with Me about it all. Read the words of My servant David in the Psalms. He didn't hold back his feelings. I can handle your anger and disappointment. I invite you to express your deepest feelings to Me without any filters! Bring Me all your loss and the intense pain of your suffering. It may take years to work through your anger, guilt, and profound grief, but it will be worth the effort. I will shoulder your hurts and use them to build something beautiful.

I want you to know that whatever you face, with My help, you can restore your life. But once I begin My work in you, you will never be the same person again. The power of My transforming love will use your brokenness and pain to shape your life into something healthier and more beautiful. I will gather the shattered pieces in your life and use them to refocus your priorities. I will surround you and secure you in the love of your family and truest friends. I will show you how to be transparent with the scars and mended cracks of your own life so you can see and help heal the wounds of those around you.

I am always calling you and encouraging you to let go and have faith in Me. Cry out to Me and know I have never forsaken you. Don't ever believe that I'm unwilling to forgive you or that I would not love you because of what you've been through. Let My love teach you and help you deal with your inadequacies and shortcomings. Submit to My resurrection power, and let Me piece together your life of broken colors to create a beautiful new mosaic that the world has never seen.

Seek Me with your whole heart, and let My love renew those damaged places. Remember, I am the Divine Artist who deals in resurrection and restoration. I promise to take your shattered hopes and dreams and use them to build a better life for you.

SCRIPTURE

Call on me when you are in trouble, and I will rescue you, and you will give me glory.

PSALM 50:15

The sacrifice you desire is a broken spirit. You will not reject a broken and repentant heart, O God.

PSALM 51:17

Since God chose you to be the holy people he loves, you must clothe yourselves with tenderhearted mercy, kindness, humility, gentleness, and patience. Make allowance for each other's faults, and forgive anyone who offends you. Remember, the Lord forgave you, so you must forgive others.

COLOSSIANS 3:12-13

REFLECTION

When life brings brokenness, we so often forget we serve a God who is in the restoration business! Too often, we aren't honest with Christ about the weight of our brokenness when we come face-to-face with it in our own lives. The Bible tells us that He is always working to make things new. He is like the artist who takes broken pottery pieces and mends them with gold, making them even more beautiful than the original. Have you been honest about your feelings with Jesus? What brokenness in your life do you need to surrender to Him today? How has He already made the broken places of your life shine with His life-light? How can you use your brokenness to help others carry their own burdens?

DAILY PRAYER

Lord Jesus, I do have broken areas in my life that need Your healing. Help me be honest and transparent with You. I place everything in Your artistic hands so You may make it new. Amen.

TODAY'S BLESSING

May you see your brokenness as God's grace-filled opportunity to take your life and make it beautiful. May you be a living example of Christ's resurrection art. May His work in your life be apparent to everyone this day.

THIRTY-TWO

EVEN IN THE DARKNESS

INVOCATION

Dear Jesus, may I be *still* and *aware* of Your enduring promise
to me as I abide with You in this Holy Now.

Perhaps you had a restless night and felt the weight of the
world on your shoulders as you tossed and turned. Maybe
life's circumstances have drained the light from your day.
My child, I Am the Creator of all things, including the darkness. I Am the sovereign King, and when you are part of My
Kingdom, there is nothing that can separate us. Not only will
I walk with you through the valley of the shadows in your
heart, but I am also present and attentive to you under the
darkness of the night when you most need sleep and restoration. When darkness causes fear and uncertainty, I promise to
use that darkness for My purposes. There will be times when
the dark is necessary so that you may receive much-needed
renewal and rest.

I am present in every shade of darkness. I am sovereign over all creation, both the light and the dark. I Am the One who fills the night sky with countless stars; My hand holds the sun as it sets and the moon as it rises. All you see is orchestrated by Me. In the dark, there is no need to feel isolated and alone. Let Me help you befriend the night and recognize My presence that permeates everything with My resurrection hope.

Even as uninvited thoughts disrupt your sleep, do not be afraid. As the darkness envelops you, let your soul abide in My love and rest. Remember, I created the day and night for specific purposes. You work hard in the light and renew yourself in the quiet of the dark. In those silent moments, do not be afraid; I am always watching over you as you sleep. Release all your cares to Me, and let your body recover as you lie in bed.

And in the circumstances of life when light becomes a stranger, remember that I have overcome the worst that you could face. I am sovereign, and I will hold your precious hand even in the valley full of shadows and hardship. I will use those difficulties to produce beautiful spiritual growth in you. I will be there to comfort you no matter how long the darkness persists.

When you are tempted to run from the darkness, My child, take hold of the good news that nothing can separate you from My love. There is no darkness that I will not use to perfect you or renew you. I will be there to use all things for My glory and purpose. So lay your head down and sleep well, even on the most anxious nights, knowing I am watching over you. I Am the Beginning and the End, the King of Kings, and the Lover of your soul. I am perfecting you in My love, working even in the darkness.

SCRIPTURE

Even in darkness I cannot hide from you. To you the night shines as bright as day. Darkness and light are the same to you.

PSALM 139:12

"Can anyone hide from me in a secret place? Am I not everywhere in all the heavens and earth?" says the LORD.

JEREMIAH 23:24

Give all your worries and cares to God, for he cares about you.

I PETER 5:7

REFLECTION

We often think of darkness only in negative terms. But the Bible is clear that Christ is present with us through every part of life—and that includes the darkness. He walks with us through the shadowy difficulties of life and uses those trials and tribulations to perfect us and bring us closer to Him. He is also with us in the actual darkness of night when most of us are sleeping, a natural state so necessary to rejuvenate our bodies and restore our spirits. Consider how Christ has used the shadowy and challenging times in your life to bring you closer to Him. Do you rest well at night knowing that Christ made the darkness for your renewal? In what areas of darkness do you lose faith in Christ's sovereignty?

DAILY PRAYER

Lord Jesus, help me lie down and rest in You. I release my fears and anxiety, focusing my eyes upon Your Kingdom as I trust in You for renewal. Give me faith that You are working to bring me closer to You through the dark and difficult times of life as well. As I inhale, I breathe in Your loving-kindness for me. As I exhale, I release the thoughts troubling my soul. With each breath I take, comfort me with Your eternal presence in the darkness. Amen.

TODAY'S BLESSING

May you rest in the knowledge that Christ is Ruler over all creation—even the darkness. May you boldly proclaim victory when you are faced with the shadows that life brings. May you be renewed in the darkness of night so you may shine for Christ in the day.

THIRTY-THREE

I AM THE FINAL ANSWER

INVOCATION

Dear Jesus, may I be *still* and *aware* of Your enduring promise to me as I abide with You in this Holy Now.

When you find yourself searching and grasping for the right answers and your life seems frayed and confusing, don't deplete your valuable energy by looking for resolutions apart from Me. The world may offer you this quick solution or that shortcut, but you will surely find those answers temporary and unsuccessful. I invite you to come into My presence for help before you go anywhere else. Find a quiet place where you can be still and pray and listen for My voice. My child, I am always there, waiting for you in that solitude. And My promise to you is that I will always have the answer that is best for you no matter your question. What the world offers will always fall short, but My answers will be the foundation to an eternally rich life. My child, learn to quiet your mind, hear My voice, and follow Me in confidence.

Be wary of laboring and stressing over tough decisions, which can negatively impact your emotional health and well-being. It is natural for your mind to race, thinking about all the possibilities . . . from the hopeful outcomes to the potential disasters. I know that some of this turmoil you feel is because you carry the weight of how your decisions may impact everyone else in your life. But remember that your fears and your anxiety do not add another second to your life! I do not want you to worry about tomorrow because today will always have enough of its own concerns. You accomplish nothing with all that energy except to project yourself away from My presence in this moment and into an unlived future. You must simply learn to bring your awareness to Me so that I can move alongside you and give you My wisdom and strength. My child, it will take some time to learn, but there is no need to agonize over your problems alone.

I always want the best possible outcome for you, not unlike a parent who responds to their child when he needs help or guidance. Search your heart, and you will know how much closer I am to you than a parent. When you call My name, I will be there; My care and love will guide you to the right decisions. You are Mine, and My answers for you are always the right ones.

When you are facing any significant decision, seek My presence in the silence. You will find competent counsel through My Word and the wisdom of those who love Me. With My help, leaning on My strength, your decisions can be based not on fear but on faith and hope in Me. So dedicate yourself to studying My Word. Surround yourself with My committed followers, and listen to them because I will speak through them.

Once you understand My direction, be decisive. Make your choice, and do your best to move ahead. Let My peace permeate your soul, and trust Me to work all things for your good even when you can't comprehend the big picture. The paralysis of being indecisive can also keep your life in constant turmoil. Most things won't get better by waiting until tomorrow. And if you realize you have made a wrong decision, don't beat yourself up. Give yourself the same grace I give to you. Do your best, and remember that it is the intentions of your heart that count the most.

Give thanks that I am with you and will be with you through every choice you face. My presence in your life brings the reassurance and strength you need to get through each day even when you feel you are at your wit's end! That is what My grace and love are all about. I promise I have the final answer—the best one for you.

SCRIPTURE

We know that God causes everything to work together for the good of those who love God and are called according to his purpose for them.

ROMANS 8:28

If you need wisdom, ask our generous God, and he will give it to you. . . . But when you ask him, be sure that your faith is in God alone. Do not waver, for a person with divided loyalty is as unsettled as a wave of the sea that is blown and tossed by the wind. Such people should not expect to receive anything from the Lord. Their loyalty is divided between God and the world, and they are unstable in everything they do.

JAMES 1:5-8

REFLECTION

We are faced with decisions day in and day out that can seem confusing. The more responsibility we are given, the more our choices impact other people. In today's world, it can be difficult to hear Christ's voice and direction in our lives. He wants us to bring our decisions to Him. He will provide the final answer we need, if we seek Him through His Word, listen for His voice through prayer, and ask other believers for guidance. Do you seek solitude to listen for God's voice when you are faced with a tough decision? Have you surrounded yourself with other believers who can speak the wisdom of Christ into your life? Do you spend time meditating on Scripture each day so that you are better prepared to make good choices? What are the tough decisions in your life you need to hand over to Jesus today?

DAILY PRAYER

Lord Jesus, be with me in the moments where life becomes stressful and confusing. Give me the wisdom I need to trust that You have the final answer in every situation. Be present with me as I move through life's challenges and difficult choices. Open Your Word for me and show me what I need, provide wise counsel from those who follow You, and be present with me in prayer so I can clearly discern Your voice and direction. Amen.

TODAY'S BLESSING

May you make decisions today in the confidence that you have been guided through the voice of Jesus in His Word and supported by the wisdom of those who serve Him. May each decision you make reflect the resurrected Christ's redemptive work in your life, and may those choices bring the light of Jesus to all you meet today.

THIRTY-FOUR

DEATH HAS NO POWER OVER YOU

INVOCATION

Dear Jesus, may I be *still* and *aware* of Your enduring promise to me as I abide with You in this Holy Now.

My child, I have told you that your time here on earth is breathtakingly short. The writer of Ecclesiastes says a person's life is "like a vapor"—you are here today and gone tomorrow. But I have also promised that death does not have the final say. Death no longer holds any power over you. I was crucified, buried, and resurrected on the third day to conquer death's reign. If you believe in Me, you will truly live forever. And My promise of eternal life isn't something you must wait for; it begins right here and now in the very breath you take as you read My words.

So take up your cross, follow Me, and you will be released from death's final hold on you.

I have promised I will walk alongside you every step, through every new door, and be with you through every new trial. You may not have personally experienced the death of someone close to you, but death is a constant companion hovering over you and those you love. Death is near even when you are too young to see or feel it.

One day, I approached a town with My disciples where a widow was watching her only son's coffin being carried in a funeral procession. My heart immediately went out to this mother. I knew the questions she was struggling with after the difficult loss of her husband. I understood that she was grief-stricken and wondering why her son also had to die. Oh, how My heart breaks for every father and mother who loses a child! After I consoled her, I commanded the young man to get up. He immediately sat up and began to talk, and I gave him back to his mother.

Later, I mourned with Mary and Martha when their brother, Lazarus, died. He was a dear friend to Me, and I felt their distress deeply. I wept. When you are devastated by someone's death, I am fully present and share your tears. Even though I knew Lazarus was with My Father, I still cried with grief. But I wanted to demonstrate to My followers how I had been given complete authority to conquer death. I simply stood outside his tomb and shouted, "Lazarus, come out!" And My dear friend emerged in his grave clothes.

My child, I endured the cross in order to end death's grip on you. I have told you that suffering and dying are the result of a world that has fallen because of those who chose to leave the Way of Love. Your life ahead will be full of joy and pain, grief and celebration, birthdays and funerals. However, do not let the heartaches take away your zeal for living an eternal quality of life. Life is still a gift to be cherished amid all the hardship.

My child, if you believe in Me, you will someday pass from this world and into My abiding presence. In your final moments on earth, I will hold you in My arms. When the stone was rolled away from My tomb, death's final day of sovereignty in this world was ended. Death has been rendered forever powerless in the triumph of My resurrection. My promise to you was fulfilled as I rose on that third day; you and your loved ones shall live with Me beyond the grave. So go boldly into each day without fear that death has the final word. Follow Me and you can truly exclaim, "Death, where is your victory? Death, where is your sting?"

SCRIPTURE

I am the resurrection and the life. Anyone who believes in me will live, even after dying. Everyone who lives in me and believes in me will never ever die.

JOHN 11:25-26

Christ was raised from the dead, and he will never die again. Death no longer has any power over him. When he died, he died once to break the power of sin. But now that he lives, he lives for the glory of God.

ROMANS 6:9-10

REFLECTION

Sometimes, in the midst of pain and suffering, it can be difficult to remember that Christ has defeated death. If you are grieving the loss of a loved one this moment, be fully present in that grief, and know that Christ is present with you as well. Our resurrection faith does not deny death and suffering; it simply acknowledges the deep truth that death is not final for those who live in Jesus. God made us to have a relationship with one another. If someone dear to you has died, you may never be the same person again this side of eternity. Take heart; Jesus weeps with you and offers you His strength and the promise that death doesn't have the last word! How can Jesus' promise of eternal life give you courage to really live? What does it mean to you that eternal life begins right now in this moment? How has your fear of death kept you from truly living? How can you offer Christ's comfort to those who are going through this type of pain?

DAILY PRAYER

Lord Jesus, thank You for taking my sins to the cross and ending the reign of death when You rose from the grave. Help me to carry my grief for people who have died and to rejoice that they are now with You. Give me strength to reach out to others who are going through this type of sorrow. Renew my heart so that I may embrace the eternal quality of life You have promised me. Amen.

TODAY'S BLESSING

May your losses gently guide you into new ways of loving and caring for yourself and others. May you hold the promise of

Christ's abiding presence tightly even though the pathway forward is never easy. May you embrace the richness of what each moment of this life holds until the heavenly Father welcomes you home.

THIRTY-FIVE

I AM YOUR DEFENDER

INVOCATION

Dear Jesus, may I be *still* and *aware* of Your enduring promise
to me as I abide with You in this Holy Now.

When you are faced with troubles, I want you to be strong
and courageous and know that I Am your Defender. I Am
your Shield from evil when you feel helpless. I Am your
Strength when you are weak. I Am your ever-present Help in
times of trouble. When you are outnumbered, know that I
Am by your side. When your enemies come at you from every
angle and seem to be gaining ground, know that I Am in control of the battle. Take hold of the promise that I have conquered it all. No matter what conflicts you face, take refuge in
Me, your Fortress. I promise that I will fight your battles, and
I will always prevail for you.

Remember, My child, the Lord of Hosts who went

out before His chosen people into battle. It was God who drowned Egypt's armies and freed Israel from slavery. With God's strength, Joshua watched Jericho's impenetrable walls crumble into sand. With God by his side, Gideon needed only three hundred men to defeat a Midianite army of thousands. Samson called upon God to give him strength to rout the great Philistine army. With divine strength and wisdom, David was able to fell the great giant Goliath and send his army retreating in fear. And, My child, even when you face the worst the world has to offer, remember that it was I who walked through the very gates of hell, took the keys, and closed it for business. I ended death's reign over all humanity and conquered evil forever in the name of love. And I have promised that I will return and overcome all the earthly kingdoms in a show of power that will establish My throne forever.

So why do you tremble in fear when enemies form ranks against you? Why do you lack the courage to face difficulties? My child, you no longer have to defend yourself. With Me by your side, no weapon will prosper against you. You have already overcome anything the powers of this world can throw at you because I have overcome the world. That means I have won your battle against all the physical, emotional, and spiritual enemies you will ever face. Whether you are under attack at work or your enemy is a hidden addiction, I want you to call on My name when you need a Defender. I understand your inclination to fight yourself, but it will only provide these adversaries the opening they need to hurt you. Leave the fighting to Me. Embrace My love, which has conquered the world, and walk boldly into the face of conflict, knowing that love truly has the final say. When I emerged from the empty tomb, My love conquered every enemy.

When you are aligned with My purposes and are working for My Kingdom, the enemy is already defeated. When the onslaught begins, just turn your eyes toward Me. Approach even the moments that seem the most hopeless with prayer and thanksgiving because I have handed you the victory. In times of conflict, find the space to quiet your heart and mind, and you will be reminded of My enduring presence beside you. No matter where the attack is coming from, it is time to lay down your weapons, open your heart, and trust that the battle is no longer yours. I am with you and will watch over you wherever you go. Be strong and courageous, My child. Do not be afraid or discouraged. For I, the Lord Almighty, am your Defender.

SCRIPTURE

I am with you, and I will protect you wherever you go.
GENESIS 28:15

This is my command—be strong and courageous! Do not be afraid or discouraged. For the LORD your God is with you wherever you go.
JOSHUA 1:9

I can never escape from your Spirit! I can never get away from your presence! If I go up to heaven, you are there; if

I go down to the grave, you are there. If I ride the wings of the morning, if I dwell by the farthest oceans, even there your hand will guide me, and your strength will support me.

PSALM 139:7-10

REFLECTION

When we are faced with conflict or turmoil, we often forget God's role as Defender in our lives. Christ has defeated death and promises to be there with us through every challenge. We are to live with strength and courage, knowing that when we are aligned with God's love, the end of our story is already victorious. What battles have you been fighting in your life? How can you surrender to Christ and trust that He will defend you? How can you face life's challenges with the strength and courage of knowing that God goes before you? What battle do you need to claim victory over this very day?

DAILY PRAYER

Lord Jesus, help me live this day with the strength and courage of one who has been chosen by You. Forgive me for fighting my own battles and not trusting You when I am attacked by the powers of this world. I place the trials and tribulations I am facing, as well as the plans of my enemies, into Your hands. I trust You to fight my battles today. Amen.

TODAY'S BLESSING

May you be assured that the God of the universe is your
Defender this day. May you live with the confidence that your
battles have been fought and won in Christ. May you go forward in the victorious knowledge that the same Lord of Hosts
who defeated the Egyptians and the same Jesus who crushed
death with His resurrection will help you conquer whatever
challenges you face.

THIRTY-SIX

I AM YOUR GUIDING LIGHT

INVOCATION

Dear Jesus, may I be *still* and *aware* of Your enduring promise to me as I abide with You in this Holy Now.

I Am the eternal Light of the world. I was there in the beginning moments of Creation and spoke the first word that brought light into the universe. And I Am the Life-Light that moved into the neighborhood on a cold night, in a small country town so many years ago, to show you what it means to truly love and to live an eternal life. My child, as long as you look to Me, I will illuminate all your life. So take hold of My promise, and let Me be your guide.

I know this fast-paced and noisy world will seem clouded and confusing at times. Always look to My light first to clarify what is happening around you. With My brightness, you will see things as they really are and will avoid being misled. Don't try to interpret things without casting My light on the situation! The truth cannot hide in the radiance of My love-light. When your journey becomes dark, let Me shine My clarity before you on your path. I will lead you with a light even brighter than the pillar of fire that guided Israel on their journey out of slavery. Under My light, you can trust that you will be sure-footed on any path. So look to Me for guidance. Whenever things feel murky, remember I Am the Way.

And, My child, look to My light for the sustenance you need to grow and change. Just as creation needs the rays of the sun to grow strong, you need to spend time in My light to grow the deep spiritual roots that can sustain you through gray winter seasons. Look to My light, even when it is uncomfortably bright, My child, because you desperately need Me to illuminate the shadows in your own soul that need confession and My forgiveness. Allow the purity of My light to penetrate your heart so it can receive My healing. And in the times when you find yourself hungry and cold, when you are in need of warmth and love, look to My radiance, and I will be there to comfort you. My light will thaw you and embrace you and give you what you need to keep going. But My light is not just for you to hold and hide away for yourself. It is to be used as a beacon of hope to rescue others from the darkness.

My light sparks the flame inside your soul. It is a holy flame, but it is not safe. My light burns within you so that you can share it with your neighbor. Unless you can recognize even the smallest sparks of My light in all humanity, especially in your enemies, then you have not truly seen Me. My light is a sacred fire that burns everything away until there is nothing left but love. Just as you may pass candles to one another in a church service, so My love and light will spread person to person. In this way, I want you to be an agent of illumination in your neighborhood. Once My light has entered your world, there is no amount of darkness and despair that could snuff it out.

I Am the Light of salvation that brings Good News for those who live without hope. I came to heal the brokenhearted and to set the captives free. I came to release those trapped in the prison of their minds. My glory shines into the darkness beyond the outer limits of the earth. I Am the omnipotent and omnipresent Light of the entire universe. Hold My light up as you examine the world, and you will see the promise of My love for you and for all creation.

SCRIPTURE

The LORD is my light and my salvation.

PSALM 27:1

The LORD your God will be your everlasting light.

ISAIAH 60:19

I am the light of the world. If you follow me, you won't have to walk in darkness, because you will have the light that leads to life.

JOHN 8:12

There will be no night there—no need for lamps or sun—for the Lord God will shine on them.

REVELATION 22:5

REFLECTION

Scripture tells us that God spoke light into existence at the beginning of time. And Jesus consistently refers to Himself as the "light of the world." What does Jesus' claim mean to you? Do you look at the world under the light of His love? Do you interpret what is happening in your life through His light? Do you trust Him to reveal the sin in your heart with His light? Consider the places in your life where Christ's light needs to shine today. How can you share His light with someone in a practical way?

DAILY PRAYER

Lord Jesus, bring Your light into the places of my life that most need it. Make any shadows apparent to me this day. Help me see the world through Your light and be aware of where You want me to share Your love. I want to be Your light bearer and let others know what You have done. Amen.

TODAY'S BLESSING

May you burn with the life-light of the resurrected Christ today. May you be an agent of illumination for others in your neighborhood, and may the light of Christ go before you in your journey and bring you closer to Him with every step you take toward love.

THIRTY-SEVEN

I AM LORD OF YOUR WHOLE LIFE

INVOCATION

Dear Jesus, may I be *still* and *aware* of Your enduring promise to me as I abide with You in this Holy Now.

I want you to understand what it truly means to call Me Lord. I have told you that I am the good King, but I am also a King who requires your obedience. When I command you to call Me Lord, it means I want to rule over every area of your life. Remember the first commandment My Father gave to Moses and His chosen people? You must not have any other god but Me. Right now, what are you prioritizing over our relationship? Whatever you choose to place ahead of Me is a false god that will only separate you from My love. I know how easy it is for you to compartmentalize your life. You can conveniently divide it into Sundays and Mondays, work and family, private and public. But for Me to be Lord, you must surrender all those territories over to Me.

Stop believing you can divide your life into neatly divided

or separate areas—it's a dangerous illusion. I have taught you that everything is spiritual, and what you do in one part of your life will have a great impact on all the areas of your life. How you act at work will eventually affect your family. What you do at church will impact your work. What you do behind closed doors will eventually come to light in public. All your life is deeply woven together. When I say I want to be Lord over every segment of you, it is only because I desire wholeness for you, My child.

When you call Me Lord, you are saying I Am the Ruler of your entire life. When My first disciples called Me Lord, they were declaring Me to be more important than Caesar, who governed the Roman Empire at that time. I am more important than any other ruler or authority in your life. And My Kingship over you will outlast them all. As you enter into relationship with Me, you will discover that crowning Me Lord of your life is exactly what I desire for you. The unequaled power of My resurrection provides you with meaning and inner stability.

I did not go to the cross to teach you better life skills or bring you success or happiness. No, I was brutally crucified and gloriously resurrected so I could rule over your entire life. I know that it may take time to surrender everything to Me—for some people it can take an entire lifetime. But I will pursue you relentlessly. The more territory of your life you give over to Me, the more you will reflect My love. And the more you surrender to Me, the deeper your joy will be!

I Am the Lord of goodness. I want you to experience Me beyond just knowledge. When you call Me Lord and submit everything to Me, there is an intimacy created between us that will leave you safe and secure in My arms for eternity. I want you to wake up and recognize all the areas of your life that need to be handed over to Me. I am inviting you to know Me as Lord of your true self. And I will guide you step by step in that process. When you call Me Lord, you can trust I will lead and sustain you through every twist and turn in life.

You are made in My image, created to reflect My Lordship over everything you see; I will share it all with you. I want you to trust that I am always with you and that I have an eternal unfolding plan for your life. I want you to grow in communion with Me as we walk together.

SCRIPTURE

The LORD is our God, the LORD alone. And you must love the LORD your God with all your heart, all your soul, and all your strength.

DEUTERONOMY 6:4-5

There is one God, the Father, by whom all things were created, and for whom we live. And there is one Lord, Jesus Christ, through whom all things were created, and through whom we live.

I CORINTHIANS 8:6

REFLECTION

We begin our journey with Christ by accepting His grace and love into our lives. They are a gateway into His Kingdom. We were made to reflect His rule over all creation. But as we learn to call Him Lord, He requires us to give everything to Him. We are so accustomed to separating and compartmentalizing our lives. We even pretend that the physical aspects of our lives are separate from the spiritual. But Christ wants to be Lord over our entire lives. What areas of your life have you resisted giving to Him? What does it mean for you to call Christ Lord of your life? Are you holding back territories from Christ's rule? Where do you most need Christ to be Lord today?

DAILY PRAYER

Lord Jesus, please show me the areas today where You are not Lord of my life. Please direct my thoughts, words, and actions, making them reflect Your Kingship in my life and over all creation. As I surrender the territories of my life to Your Kingdom, use them as staging grounds for hope and peace and transformation in my neighborhood. Amen.

TODAY'S BLESSING

May you surrender all your life territories to the Lordship of Jesus Christ this day. May you live a Kingdom life that radiates His light into the world. May you place everything at His feet and reflect the joy, blessing, and contentment of a true servant of the Most High King.

THIRTY-EIGHT

ALWAYS KEEP YOUR EYES UP

INVOCATION

Dear Jesus, may I be *still* and *aware* of Your enduring promise to me as I abide with You in this Holy Now.

My child, each new morning is a brand-new gift from Me. I have told you there will be a time for everything in your life. You will live through so many different seasons. As it says in My Word, there will be a time to plant and a time to uproot, a time to tear things down and a time to build, a time to cry and a time to laugh, a time to mourn and a time to dance, a time to be silent and a time to speak, a time to embrace each other and even a time to quarantine. The world around you is in constant change, seeming to move faster than ever. But through all these seasons, through all the unique circumstances of life, the promise of My enduring presence will always remain steadfast for you.

I know the chaos of life can make you feel like a seasick sailor scanning the horizon and longing for solid ground. I know it can be unnerving when people come and go from your life. The world offers fleeting hope in times like these. But, My child, throughout every season, My unshakable hope remains. It is there for you to find, if you will just keep your eyes up.

During many of life's seasons, the enemy will try to convince you that hope is lost. You will face changes that bring feelings of despair. But My hope is unwavering and always present. Fix your eyes on Me. You can find My hope in even the most desperate season. It will be there whenever you quiet yourself before Me. It will be there whenever you find the stillness. My hope will be present when you are working, if you bring your awareness to the tasks at hand. Open your eyes to My purposes that are right before you. My hope is always written in My Word for you to read and study and hide away in your heart. Meditate on it day and night. My hope is apparent in the voices of my followers. Surround yourself with them. And My hope is written in all creation if you will take the time to observe it. My hope is always there if you will raise your eyes to the horizon because I Am the Beginning and the End of time.

If you were not here to praise My name, the very rocks would cry out and proclaim My holiness. You see, My child, I am bringing resurrection life to all creation. I am working to reconcile all things. My life-light shines through the darkness in even the most unusual places. Your hope should not be placed in the uncertain things of this world. It should be secured on the solid ground of My presence. Keep your eyes focused on Me, and you will find My promise.

I have commanded you to seek Me so you will find Me. Whenever you feel lost, just open your eyes and look around. Call out to Me, and I will show you resurrection hope all around you. Ask Me, and I will grow that promise deep in your soul. I know that chaotic change can leave you hanging your head. But don't let the ever-shifting circumstances of life cause you to doubt My promise. Fix your eyes on Me, and I will calm your heart and restore your faith and confidence in My enduring love for you.

SCRIPTURE

Why am I discouraged? Why is my heart so sad? I will put my hope in God! I will praise him again—my Savior and my God!

PSALM 42:11

Faith shows the reality of what we hope for; it is the evidence of things we cannot see.

HEBREWS 11:1

Let us run with endurance the race God has set before us. We do this by keeping our eyes on Jesus, the champion who initiates and perfects our faith. Because of the joy awaiting him, he endured the cross, disregarding its shame. Now he is seated in the place of honor beside God's throne.

HEBREWS 12:1-2

REFLECTION

Today's world moves at such a fast pace. By the time we have steadied ourselves in one season, we look up and find the world has already moved into another! When everything keeps changing, it is difficult to remember that Christ does not change. In a world of despair, He offers us steadfast hope no matter what we are facing. Has despair crept into your life? Where can you find hope today? What has prevented you from placing your hope in Christ? Are you in a season of life where you need to focus your vision on the promise of Christ's unchanging love?

DAILY PRAYER

Lord Jesus, remind me that Your hope is always present and available even when I cannot seem to find it. Bring my attention to the present moment, and help me see Your hope written in the world all around me. Shoulder my despair and replace it with Your resurrection love. Amen.

TODAY'S BLESSING

May you experience the abiding hope of the resurrected Jesus this day. May that hope radiate through His Word and make a difference in whatever you do today. May you see hope accented in creation's beauty, and may you have opportunities to share a message of hope with everyone you encounter. May God's eternal promise guide you and His presence comfort you.

THIRTY-NINE

I AM YOUR ADVOCATE

INVOCATION

Dear Jesus, may I be *still* and *aware* of Your enduring promise
to me as I abide with You in this Holy Now.

I know there will be times in your life when you wonder how
anyone could love you or if anyone is by your side to help
you through your troubles. There will be situations when
you make promises you won't be able to keep. You will mess
up, make mistakes, and let people down. I already know
about each of those moments when your choices have caused
even your family and friends to walk away from you. My
child, you will miss the mark and hurt people. And in these
instances, the voice of the accuser will be there to point out
everything you have done wrong. This enemy is always eager
to take advantage of your slip-ups. He wants you to believe
that you aren't worthy of My love. He will tell you that your
mistakes are unforgivable and you are doomed to a life of sin
and failure. I know how easy it will be for you to question

My presence in these dark moments. Sometimes, it will seem as if the whole world is aligned to highlight your failures and drown out the truth of My love Story. But you must know that I Am always on your side. I Am your eternal Defense Attorney, and I Am undefeated in my protection of all who cry to Me for help. My grace knows no limits. I promise that no matter what you have done, I will be there when you confess your sins and call My name.

I have already defeated that same accuser who wants you to believe that you are beyond defending. You see, I was handed over by misguided religious people to be executed by an unjust empire, even though I stood blameless before their courts. But I chose to do this so I could be your eternal Advocate. I was put on trial so you would never have to be. Yes, I stood in your place for all the times you have missed the mark in your life. Because of My sacrifice on the cross, you are forever held blameless and righteous before My Father. So do not allow your mistakes and the accusations of a defeated enemy to confuse you about My enduring love for you. And please do not let self-condemnation keep you imprisoned in guilt and shame. Believe Me when I tell you that I know the intimate details of your situation and of those you have wronged. I understand all your pain—I see your heart. I know how the enemy tries to make you feel like a worthless criminal. And I also know your desire for forgiveness and restoration.

I Am the One who will stand for you even when you lose sight of the way. In those uncertain moments, when you cannot distinguish My voice, simply trust Me, and I will save you and make you whole. When you feel you have missed the mark, call on Me, and I will forgive you and restore your hope. Never give up on yourself, because I never give up on you. Remember how the fruit of My Spirit dwells within you, even when the accuser claims you are beyond reclamation. Whenever you reach out to Me, I will be beside you, before you, and behind you. Identify and confess your faults and release them to Me. My grace and loyalty are steadfast. My love for you cannot be extinguished. My child, I will always be your Advocate.

SCRIPTURE

Pilate asked [Jesus], "Are you the king of the Jews?" Jesus replied, "You have said it."

LUKE 23:3

There is no condemnation for those who belong to Christ Jesus.

ROMANS 8:1

My dear children, I am writing this to you so that you will not sin. But if anyone does sin, we have an advocate who pleads our case before the Father. He is Jesus Christ, the one who is truly righteous.

I JOHN 2:1

REFLECTION

There are times in life when it seems as if the odds are stacked against us, when we feel attacked from every side. On top of the worldly challenges we face, the Bible tells us the enemy is an accuser who comes to steal our hope and destroy us. But we also have a holy Advocate who knows the inner workings of our hearts. He was accused and condemned even though He was innocent. Because of His sacrifice, we are held blameless and holy in the eyes of God. Do you need Christ to be your Advocate today? How have the enemy's accusations tried to separate you from Christ's love? What do you need to confess to Christ in order for Him to represent you? What areas of your life do you need to entrust to Christ?

DAILY PRAYER

Lord Jesus, forgive my sins today and plead my case before the Father to prove me innocent in the face of my accusers. Remind me to come to You when I feel alone and under attack. Give me strength and courage and cover me in Your grace so that I may be holy and blameless in the sight of God. Amen.

TODAY'S BLESSING

May you never feel abandoned but cling to the assurance that you have a holy Advocate by your side. May you call on the name of Christ to defend you against the accuser and the world's army of prosecutors. May you live boldly because you are made holy and blameless by Christ's death and resurrection.

FORTY

THE GOOD NEWS: I WILL ABIDE IN YOU

INVOCATION

Dear Jesus, may I be *still* and *aware* of Your enduring promise to me as I abide with You in this Holy Now.

I want to remind you of the truest Story. Not just the story of the world but the Story about you and Me. Remember how I breathed life into Adam at the dawn of history before sin separated us? And recall how I took on flesh and blood, all because of you? I taught you how to love. When I went to the cross to finish My work of reconciliation, I tore the Temple veil in half, removing the barrier between us. I was no longer going to tolerate being kept apart from you. I was no longer going to be held in a man-made temple. You, My child, in that very moment, became My temple. As you breathe in and out and read these words, you should know that your breath comes from Me. And now that you have given your life to Me, I will always abide in you.

The religious people may say that I am just waiting to meet you in some building at a particular time of day. But that is not the true Story. The in-crowd may say I am hovering off in the distance until you say some specially arranged words to make Me appear. That is not My Good News. And I am also not hidden away in some holy city or far-off destination. You do not need to travel long distances to find Me. I Am the God who is on the move *with* you. I am with you every moment of the day, including right now.

It is time for you to take hold of the resurrection power inside of you. I breathed My Spirit on My disciples and sent them out into the world. I told you that whoever believes in Me will not just do the works that I did in My earthly ministry—even greater things than that are possible through you! My Spirit descended as fire on everyone gathered on the day of Pentecost, and continues to be poured out on everyone who comes to Me since that day. You are My new address, My dwelling place in this Holy Now.

Each person who believes in Me has the Spirit of God living in them and is a child of God. The keys of My Kingdom are given to all of you who are united as one in Me. I have chosen you specifically to be an integral part of My body, and so your earthly body is the dwelling place of My presence. Your body is My temple, where I reside. Care for it as much as possible.

Carry yourself with grace and dignity, and do not allow anyone to degrade or shame you, for you were created in My image. You are not damaged goods. You are never unlovable. Do not waste time with self-hatred. Do not spend time beating yourself up over your mistakes. Never lose faith that anything is possible with My Spirit abiding in you.

My presence is a limitless treasure dwelling within you. My

Spirit loves you unconditionally, accepts you just as you are, and believes in you despite your weaknesses and failures. I am with you always—your Companion, your Lover, your Advocate, and your Defender. That, My child, is our true Story.

SCRIPTURE

I tell you the truth, anyone who believes in me will do the same works I have done, and even greater works, because I am going to be with the Father.

JOHN 14:12

Don't you realize that all of you together are the temple of God and that the Spirit of God lives in you? God will destroy anyone who destroys this temple. For God's temple is holy, and you are that temple.

1 CORINTHIANS 3:16-17

You are all children of God through faith in Christ Jesus. And all who have been united with Christ in baptism have put on Christ, like putting on new clothes. There is no longer Jew or Gentile, slave or free, male and female. For you are all one in Christ Jesus.

GALATIANS 3:26-28

REFLECTION

How often do you consider the scriptural truth that we are the actual temple and residence of Christ's Spirit? When you wrestle with self-worth, do you consider that Christ lives in you? Do you truly care for your body in a way that honors God's Spirit within you? How can understanding the power of Christ's Spirit dwelling in you change the way you see your work and your relationships? What are some areas of your life where you need to recognize and claim the power of the Holy Spirit?

DAILY PRAYER

Lord Jesus, please make me aware of Your presence within me today. Thank You for Your work on the cross to break through the veil of sin that separated us. I am humbly grateful that You are now dwelling in me. Help me to remember our Love Story and to allow Your Spirit to do wondrous things through me. Amen.

TODAY'S BLESSING

May you live today knowing that God's Spirit is in you. May you look upon yourself with the same love and compassion that Christ, who resides in you, surely does. May you journey through life secure in the knowledge that you are never truly alone. May you confidently live the Good News that Christ died for you, Christ rose for you, and Christ will come again.

About the Authors

Paul Bane is the founder of Mindful Christianity, an online community helping people discover the lost contemplative and meditative tradition of practicing the presence of Jesus in our daily lives. Founded in 2015, Mindful Christianity now reaches over a million people a day, and its message has connected with faith leaders in every denomination of Christianity as well as mental health professionals and counseling organizations. Paul is the retired senior pastor of New Hope Community Church in Brentwood, Tennessee. He and his wife, Cathy, have two grown children and six granddaughters.

Matt Litton is an author, a bestselling collaborative writer, and an occasional blogger. He has written for CNN, *Christianity Today*, Dallas Morning News, *Relevant*, Busted Halo, Catalyst Leader, and Mindful Christianity. He is the author of *Holy Nomad* (Abingdon Press) and *The Mockingbird Parables* (Tyndale House). He currently lives in Nashville, Tennessee, with his wife, Kristy, and their four children.

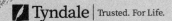